FOR ORGANS, PIANOS & ELECTRONIC KEYBOARDS

E-Z PLAY TODAY

296

Best of Cole Porter

CONTENTS

ISBN: 978-0-7935-9985-1

HAL•LEONARD®
CORPORATION
7777 W. BLUEMOUND RD. P.O. BOX 13819 MILWAUKEE, WI 53213

Visit Hal Leonard Online at
www.halleonard.com

Anything Goes

Registration 2
Rhythm: Fox Trot or Swing

Words and Music by
Cole Porter

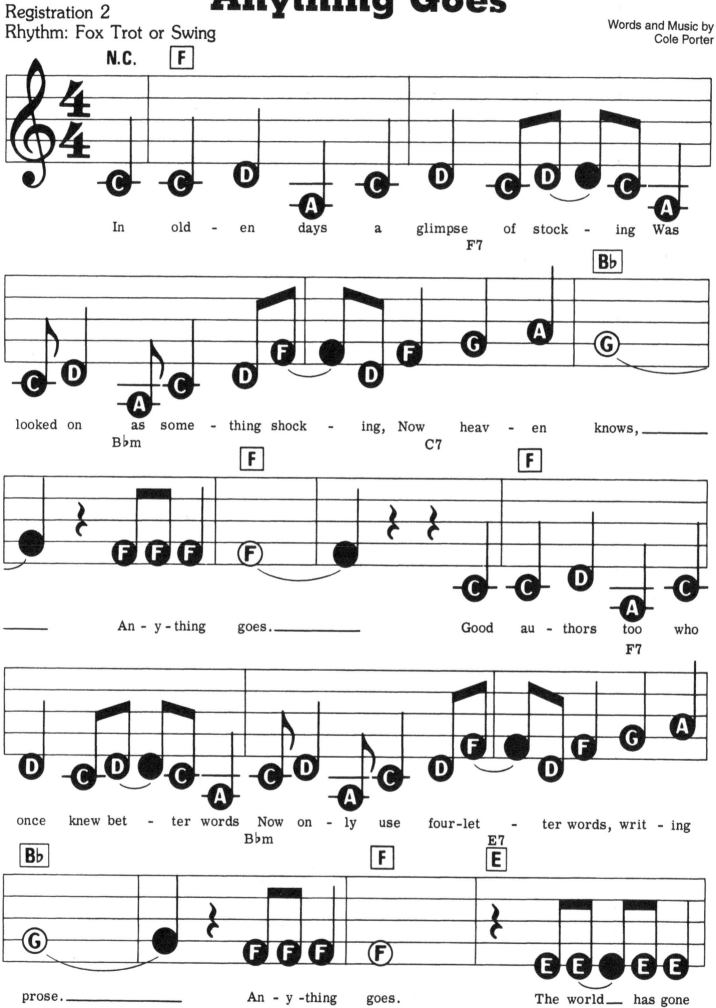

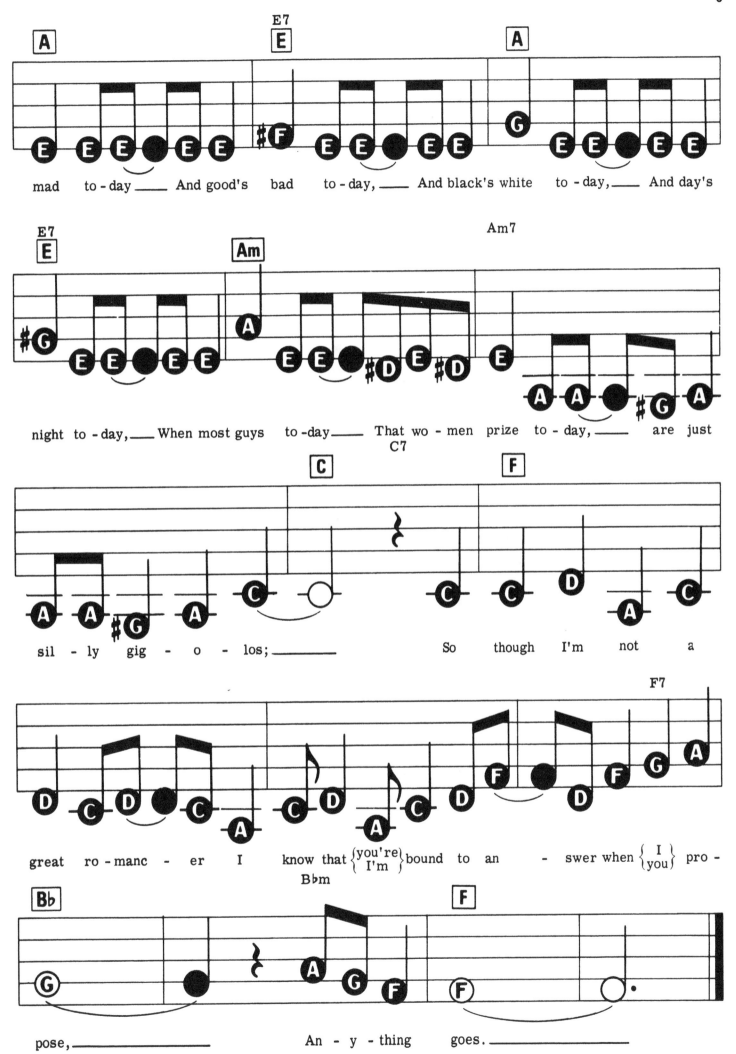

Begin the Beguine
from JUBILEE

Registration 2
Rhythm: Latin or Beguine

Words and Music by
Cole Porter

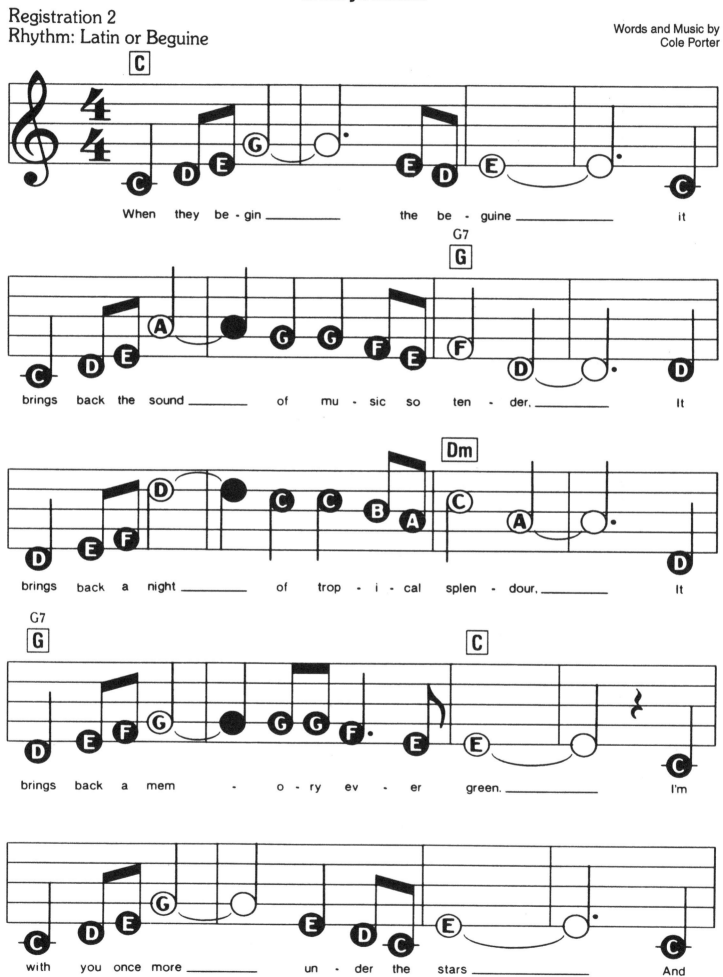

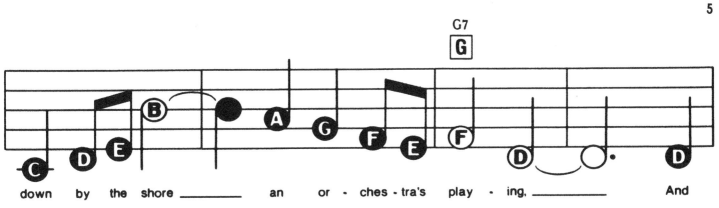

down by the shore ____ an or-ches-tra's play-ing, ____ And

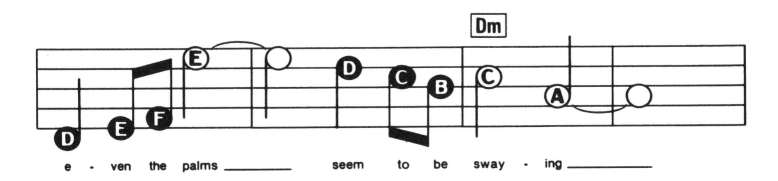

e - ven the palms ____ seem to be sway-ing ____

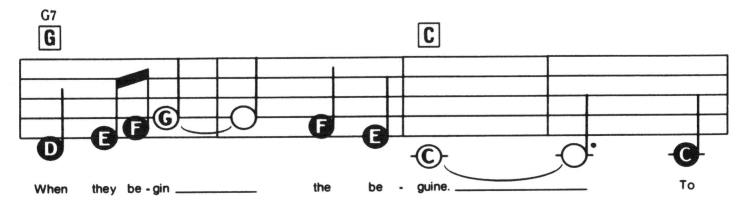

When they be-gin ____ the be-guine. ____ To

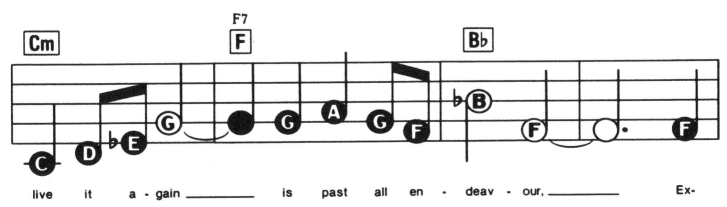

live it a-gain ____ is past all en-deav-our, ____ Ex-

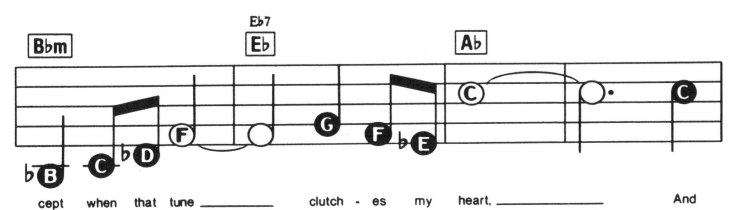

cept when that tune ____ clutch-es my heart, ____ And

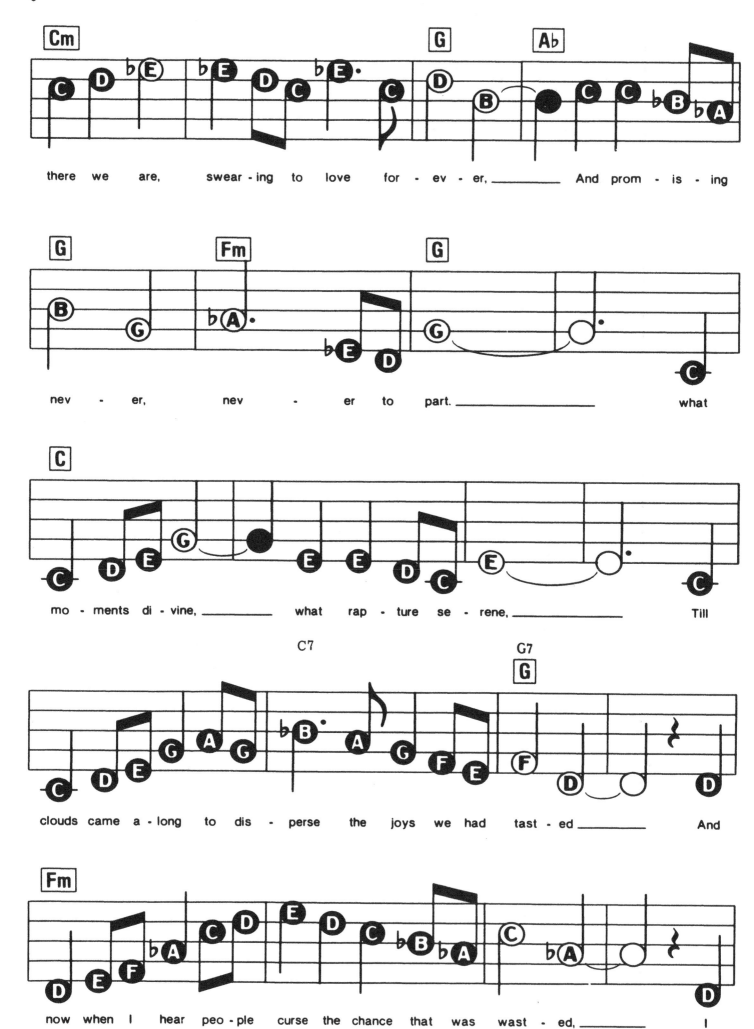

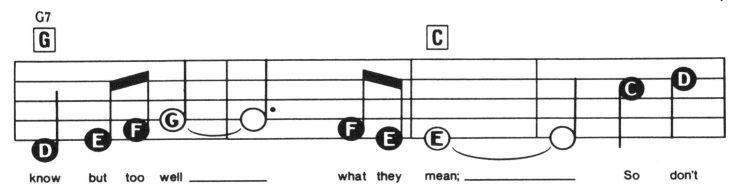

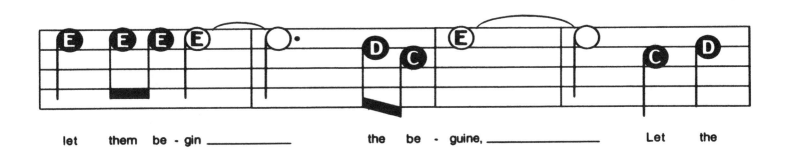

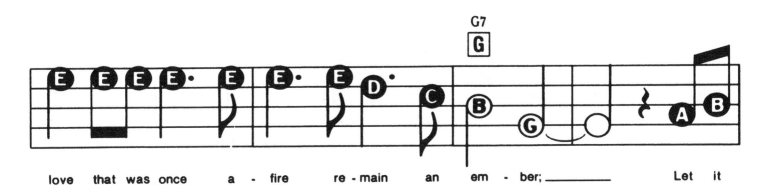

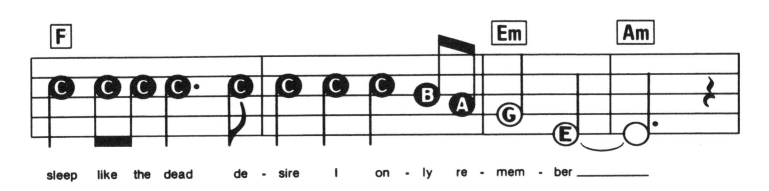

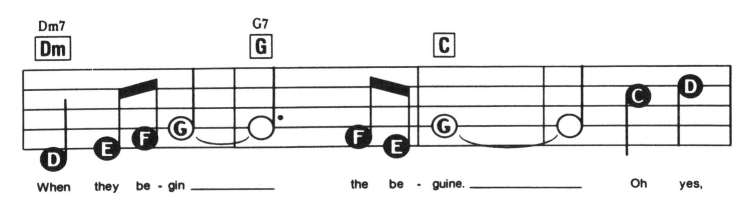

It's All Right with Me
from CAN-CAN

Registration 3
Rhythm: Swing or Fox Trot

Words and Music by
Cole Porter

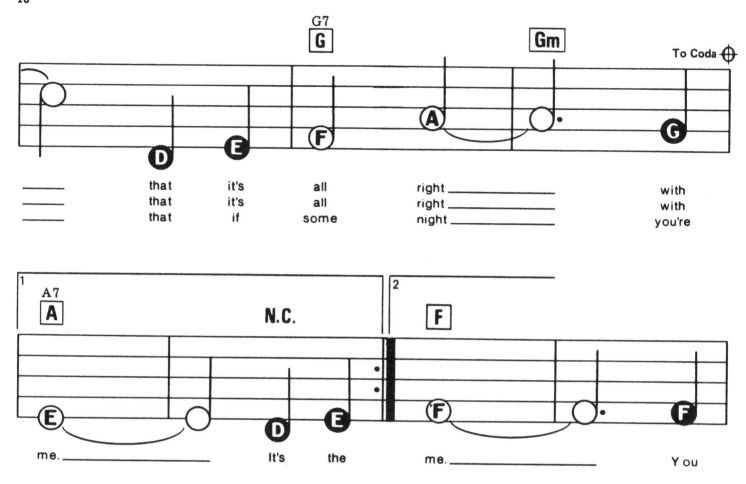

that   it's   all   right _____   with
that   it's   all   right _____   with
that   if   some   night _____   you're

me. _____   It's   the   me. _____   You

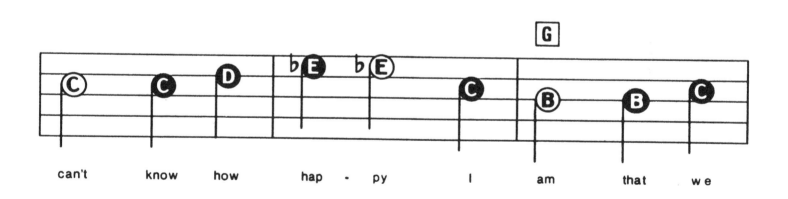

can't   know   how   hap - py   I   am   that   we

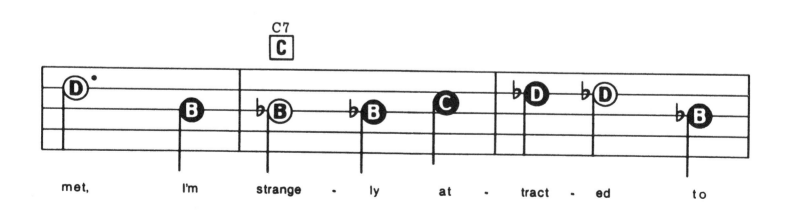

met,   I'm   strange - ly   at - tract - ed   to

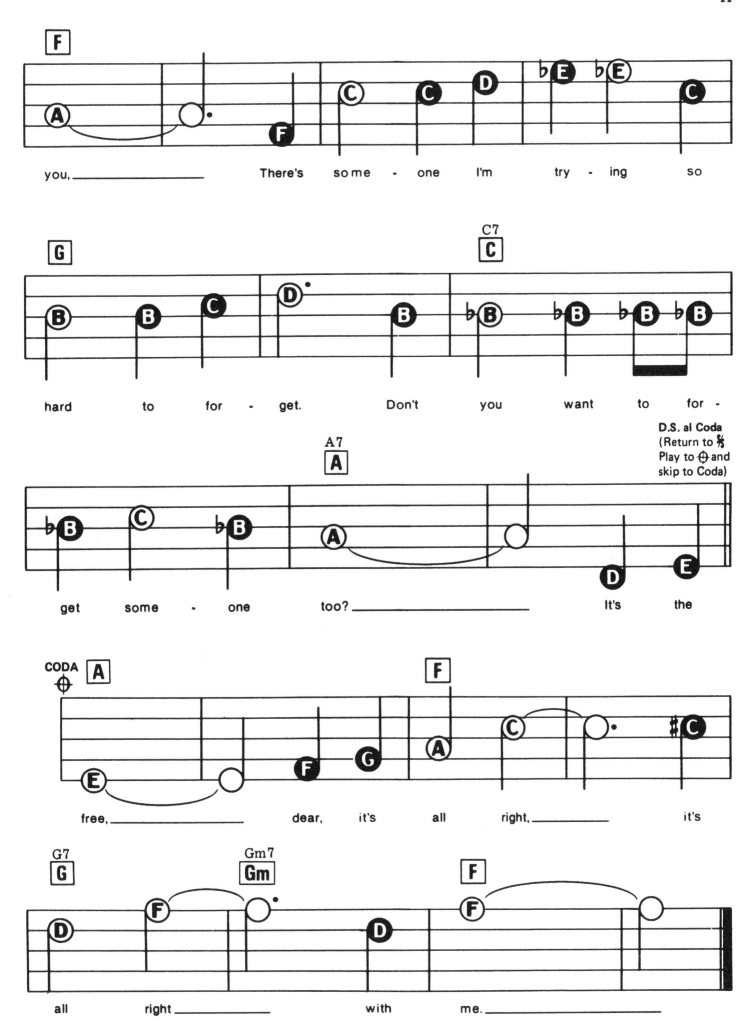

Don't Fence Me In

Registration 8
Rhythm: Fox Trot or Ballad

Words and Music by
Cole Porter

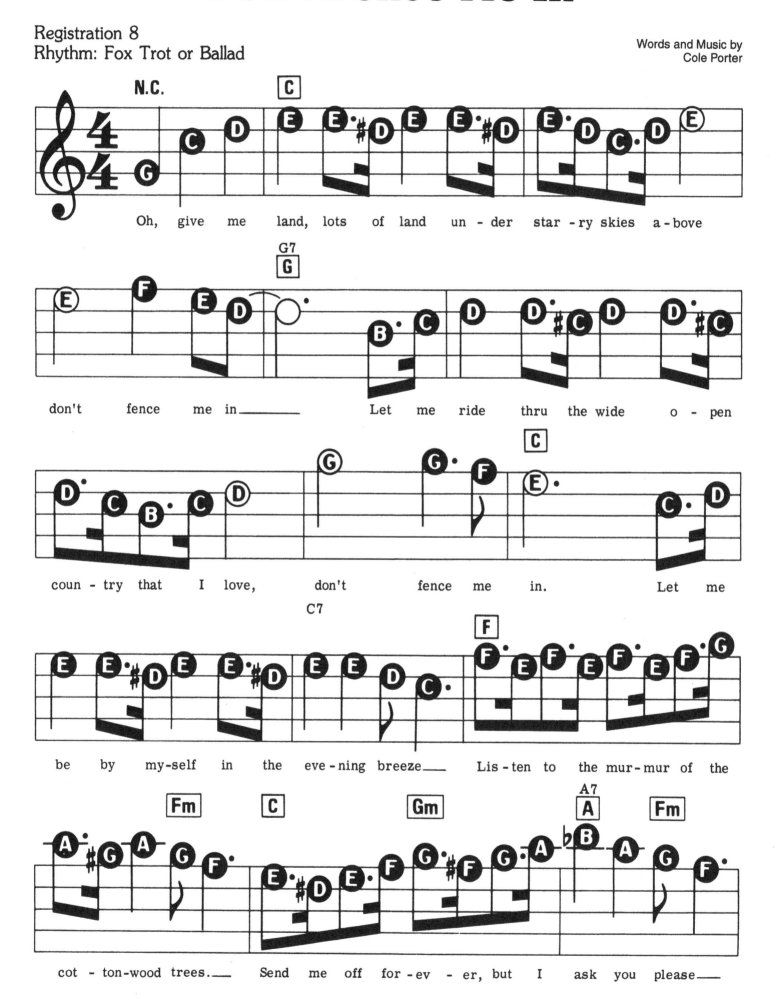

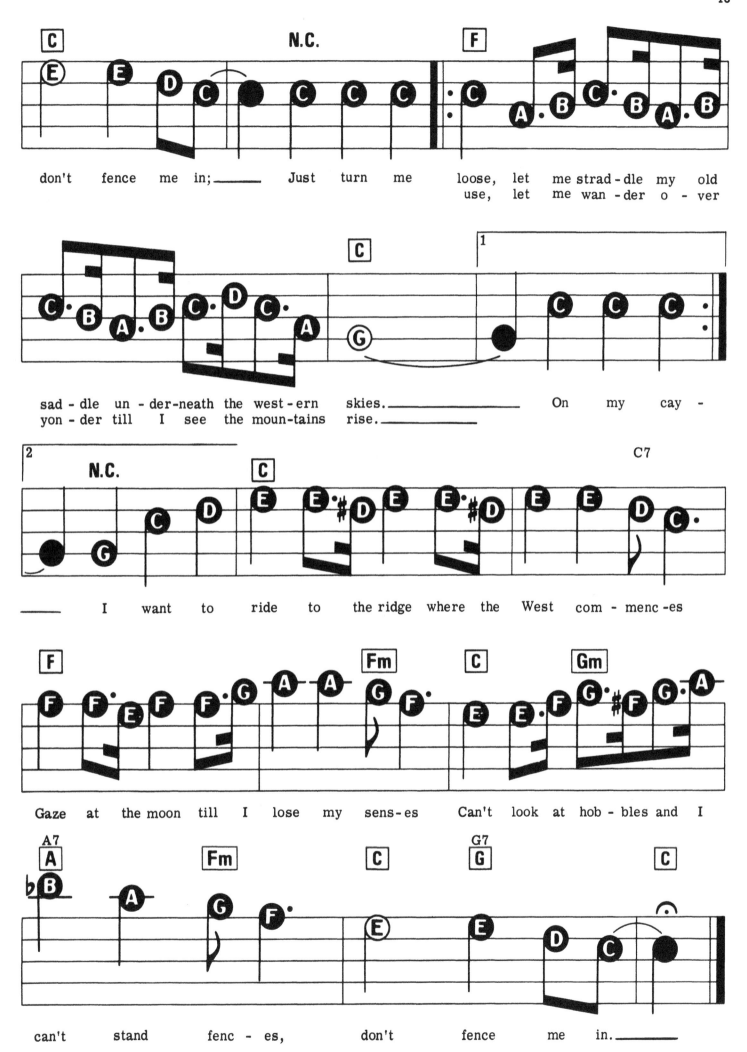

Easy to Love
(You'd Be So Easy to Love)
from BORN TO DANCE

Registration 3
Rhythm: Swing or Fox Trot

Words and Music by
Cole Porter

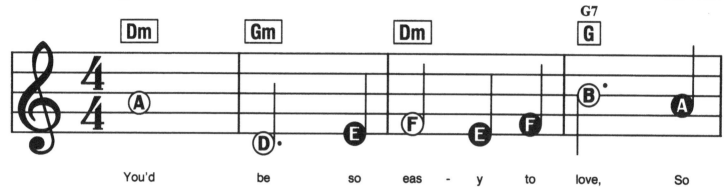

You'd be so eas - y to love, So

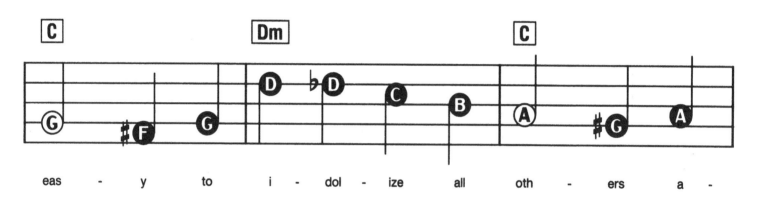

eas - y to i - dol - ize all oth - ers a -

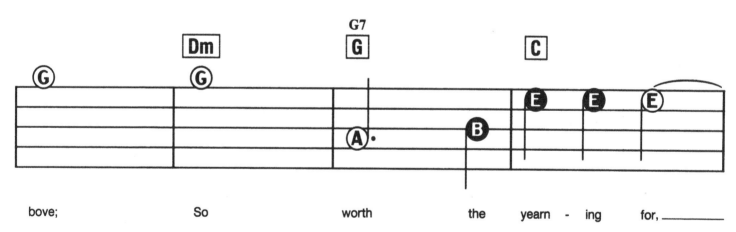

bove; So worth the yearn - ing for, _____

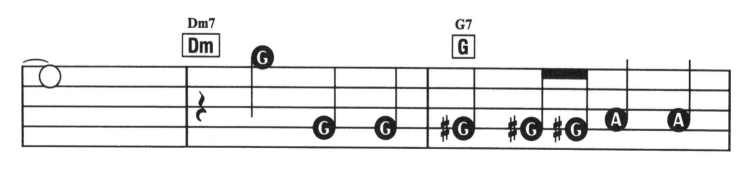

_____ So swell to keep ev - 'ry home - fire

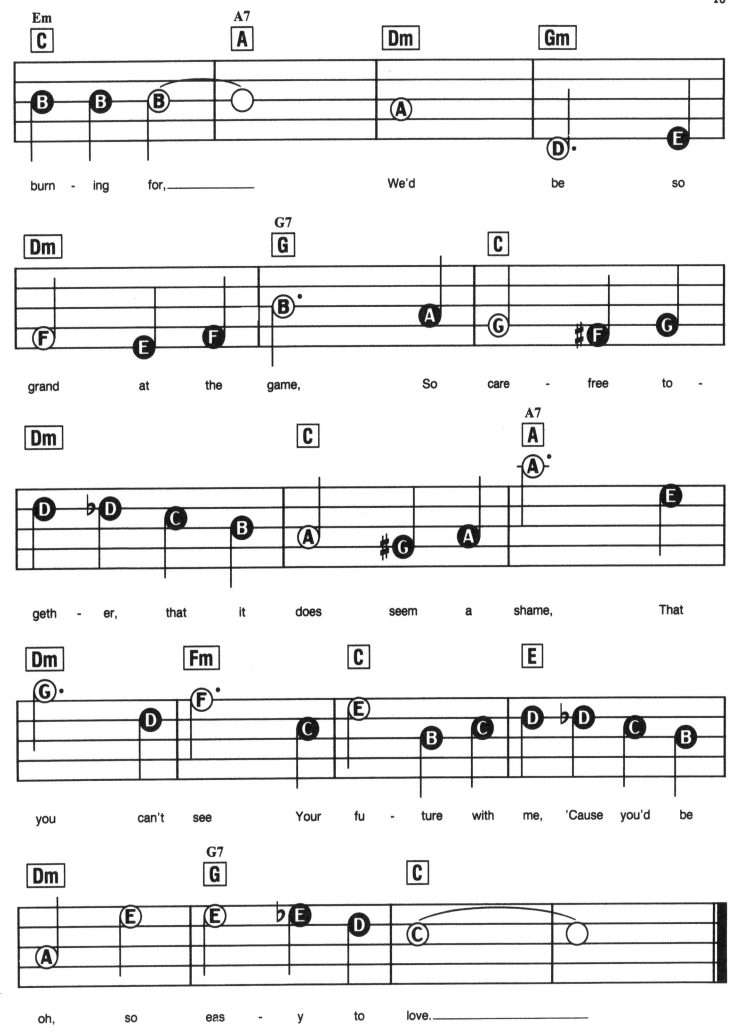

From This Moment On

from OUT OF THIS WORLD

Registration 5
Rhythm: Swing

Words and Music by
Cole Porter

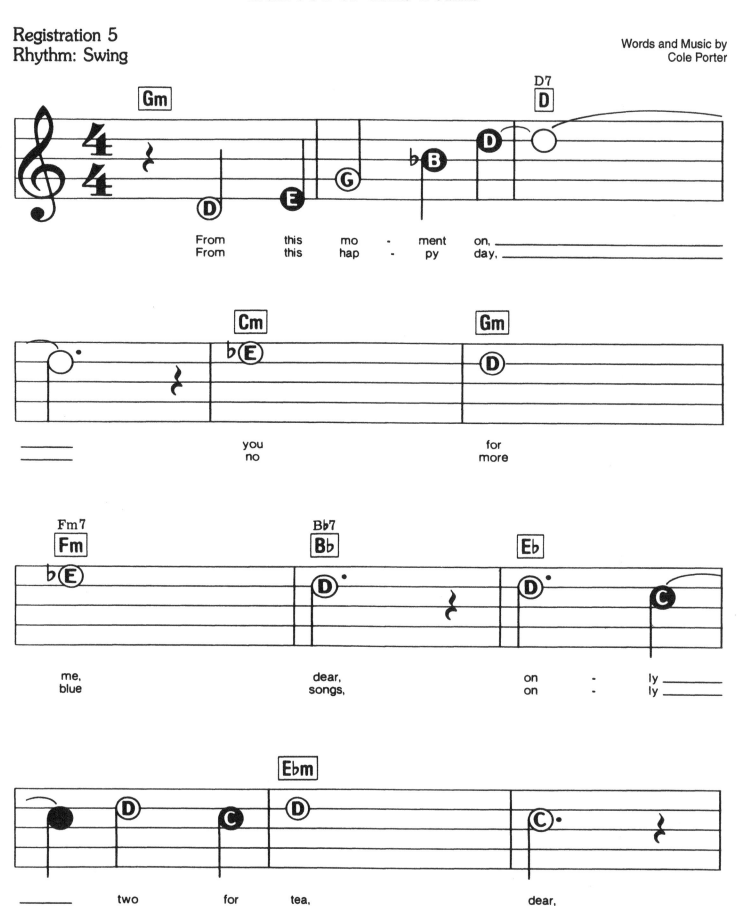

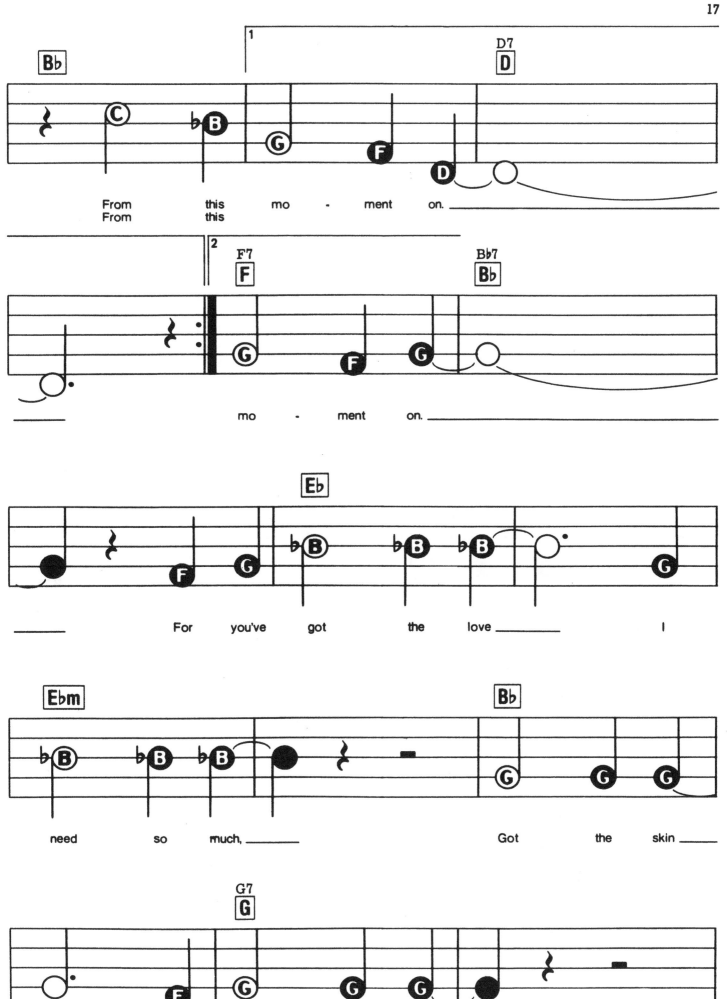

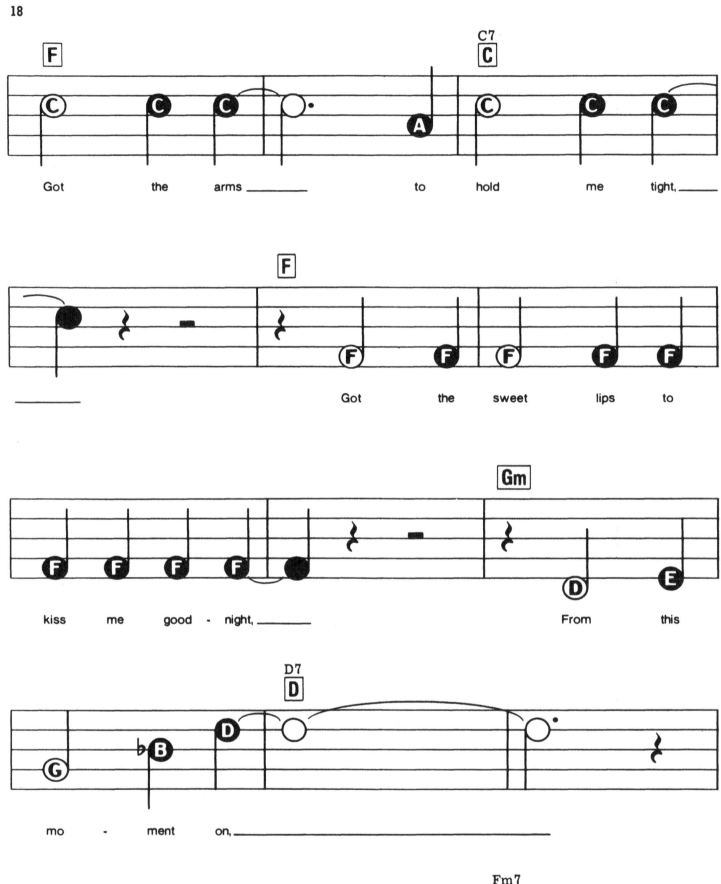

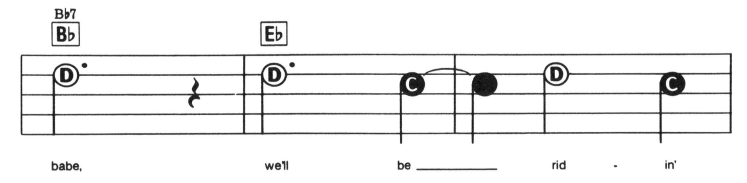

babe,   we'll   be _____ rid - in'

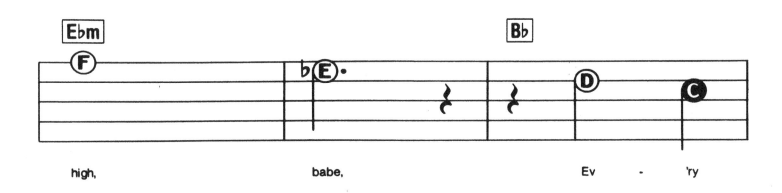

high,   babe,   Ev - 'ry

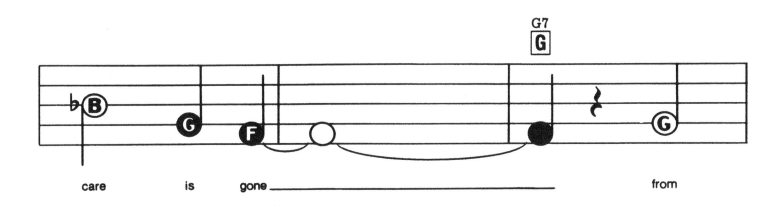

care   is   gone _____ from

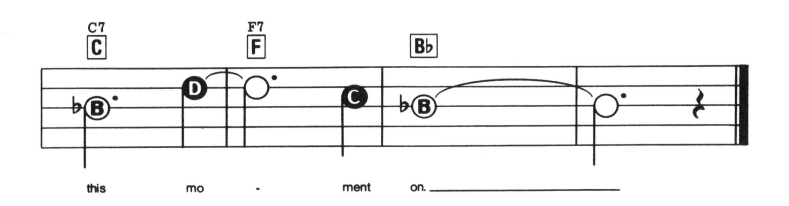

this   mo - ment   on. _____

I Concentrate on You
from BROADWAY MELODY OF 1940

Registration 1
Rhythm: Latin

Words and Music by
Cole Porter

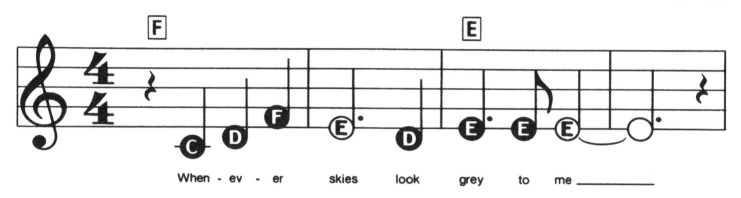

When - ev - er skies look grey to me _____

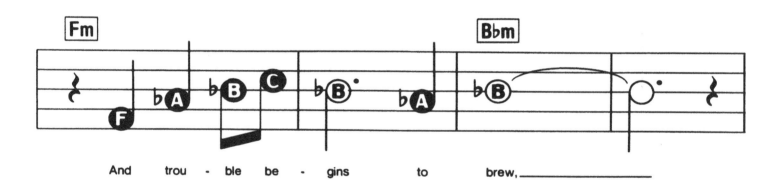

And trou - ble be - gins to brew, _____

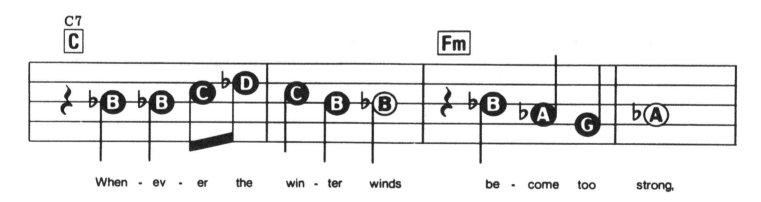

When - ev - er the win - ter winds be - come too strong,

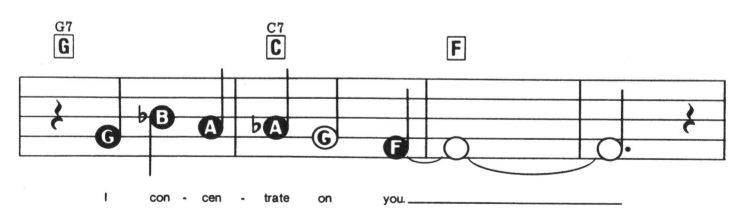

I con - cen - trate on you. _____

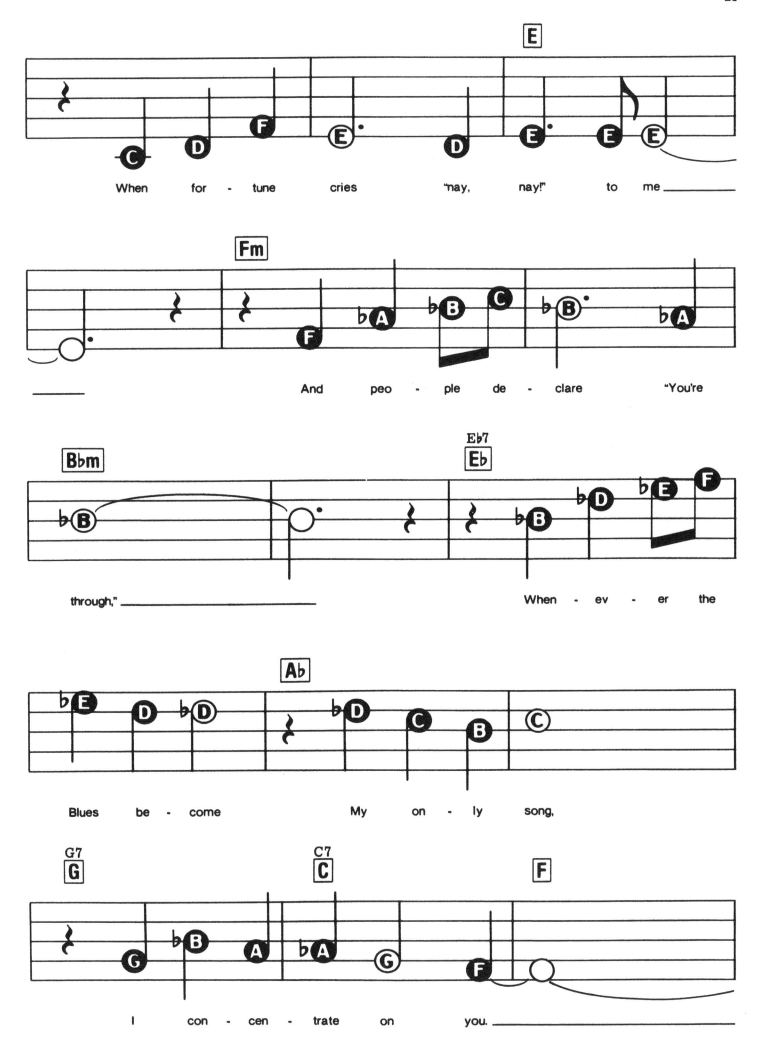

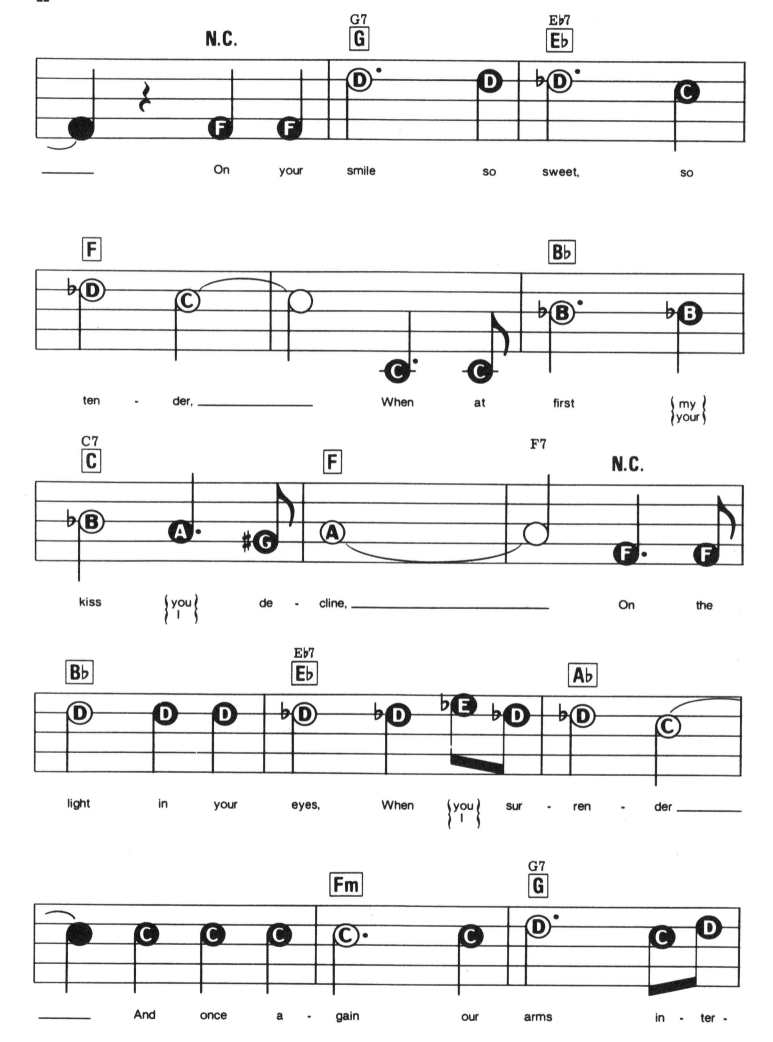

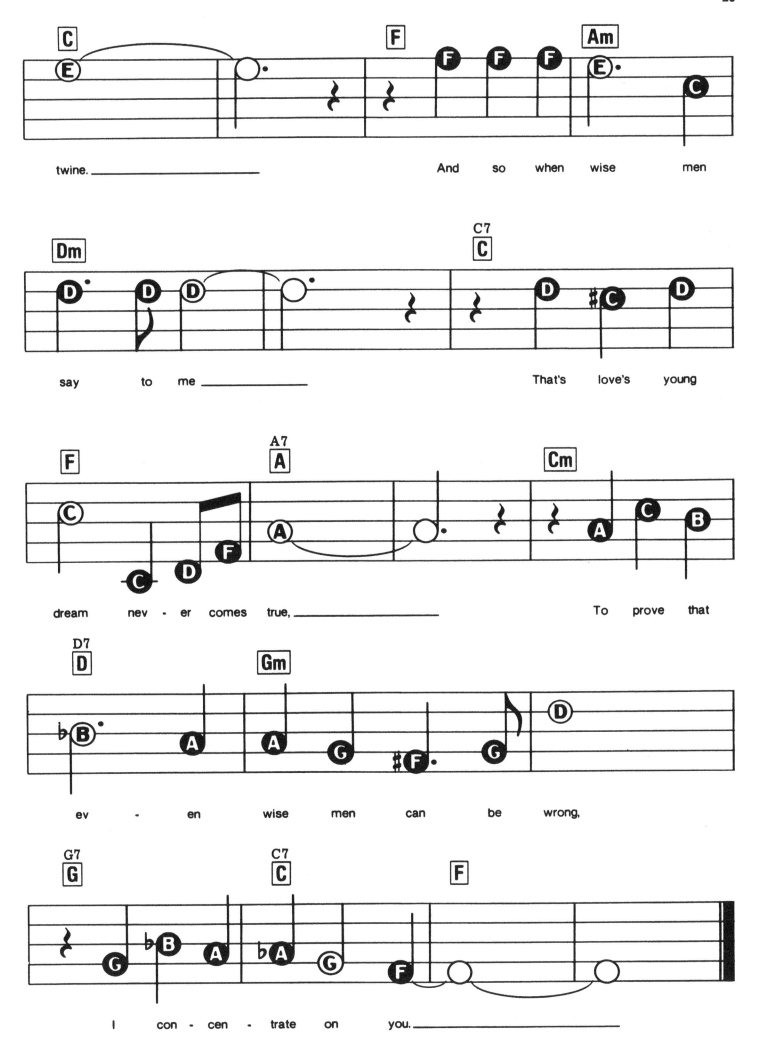

I Get a Kick out of You
from ANYTHING GOES

Registration 4
Rhythm: Fox Trot or Swing

Words and Music by
Cole Porter

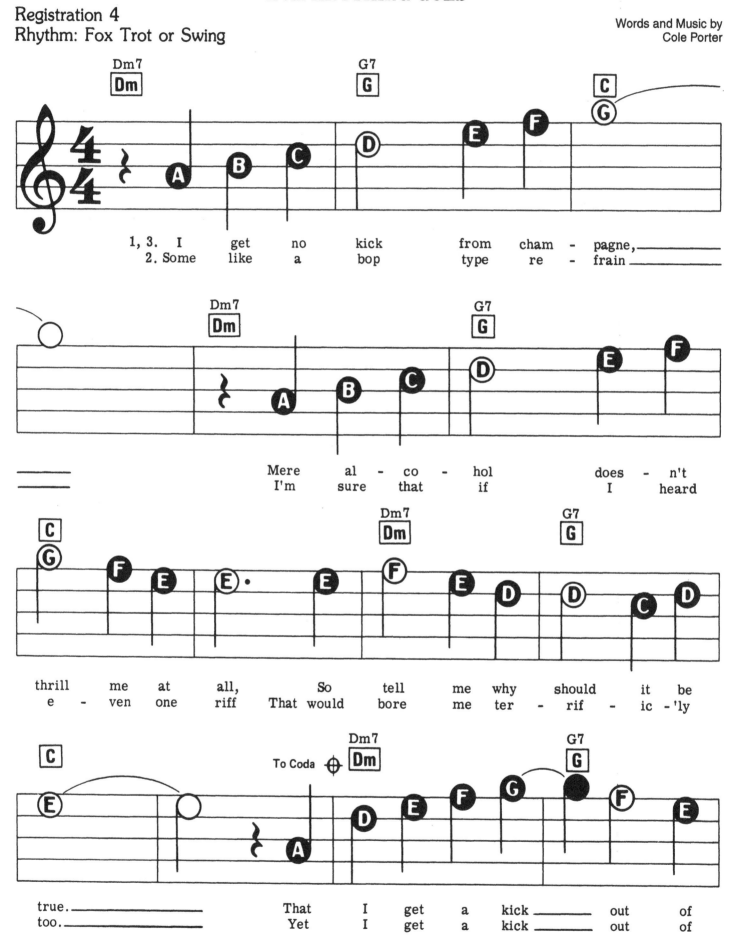

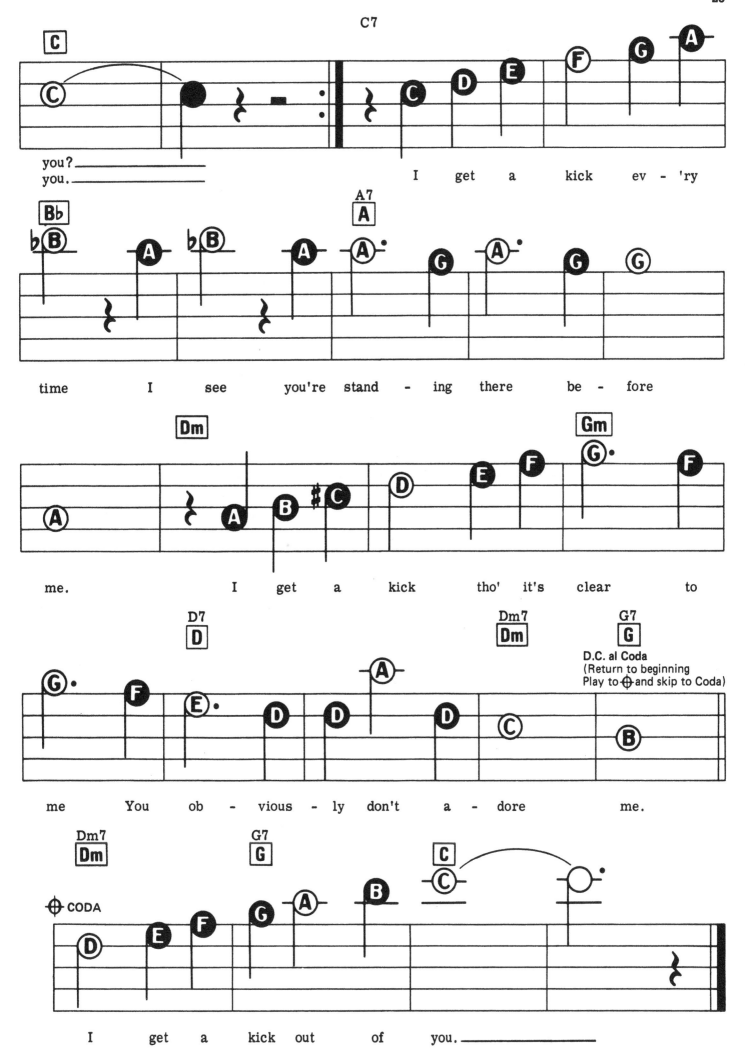

I Love Paris
from CAN-CAN

Registration 9
Rhythm: Fox Trot

Words and Music by
Cole Porter

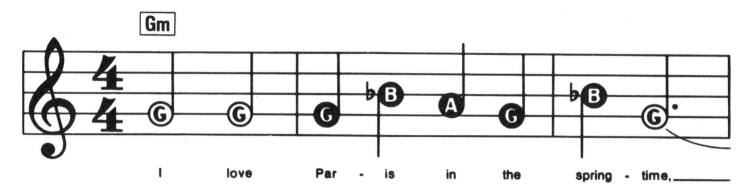

I love Par - is in the spring - time,

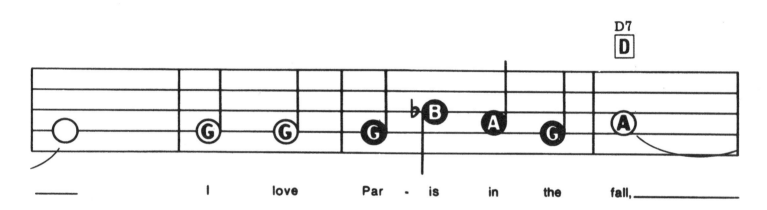

I love Par - is in the fall,

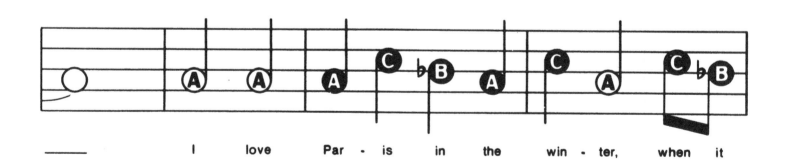

I love Par - is in the win - ter, when it

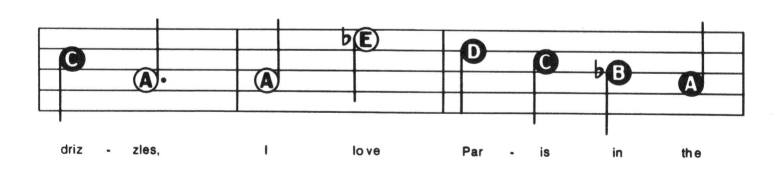

driz - zles, I love Par - is in the

27

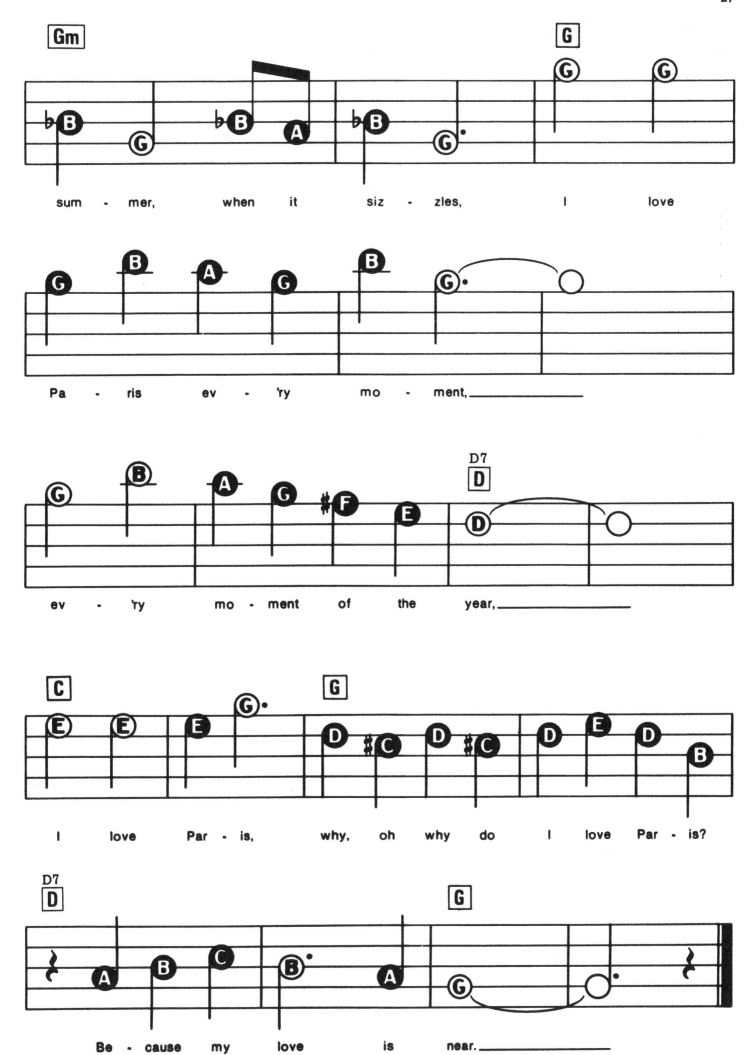

I've Got You under My Skin
from BORN TO DANCE

Registration 5
Rhythm: Ballad or Fox Trot

Words and Music by
Cole Porter

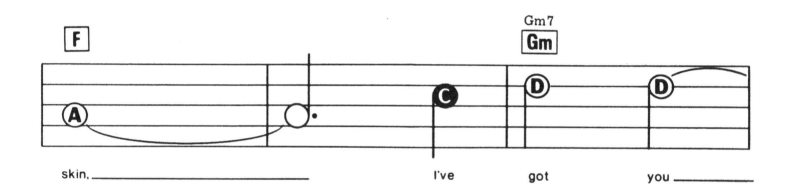

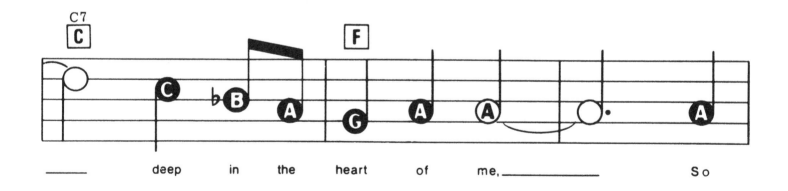

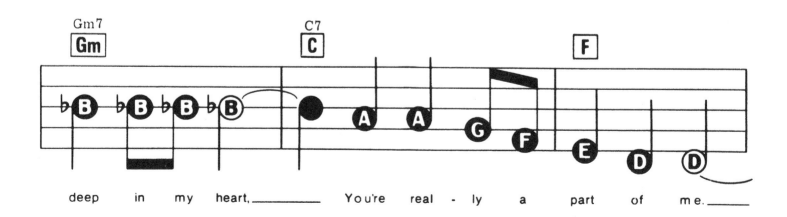

I've got you _____ un - der my skin. _____ I tried so _____ not to give in, _____ I

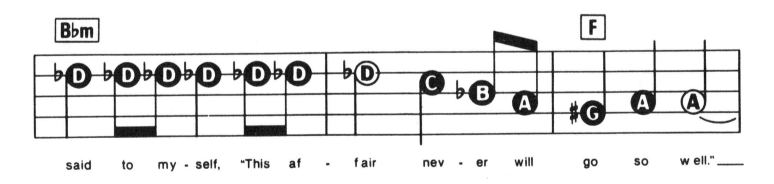

said to my - self, "This af - fair nev - er will go so well." ____

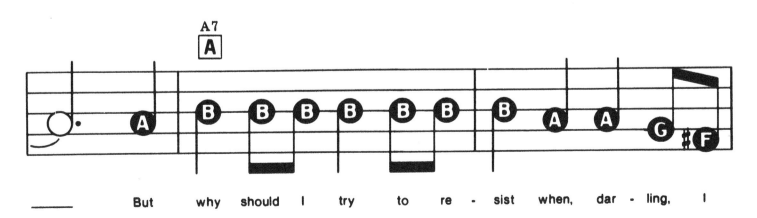

____ But why should I try to re - sist when, dar - ling, I

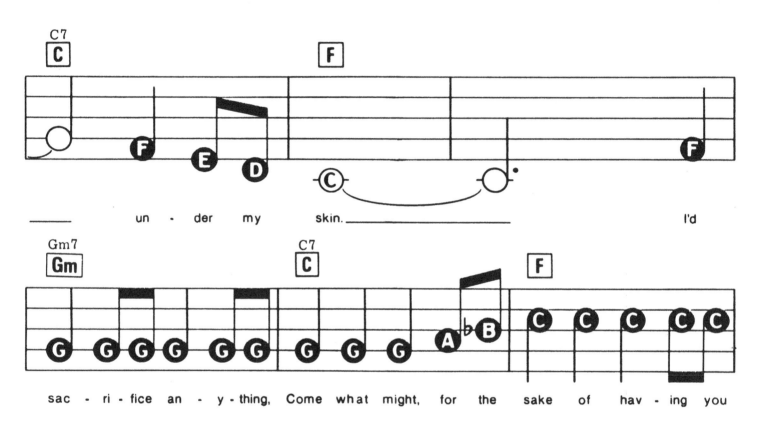

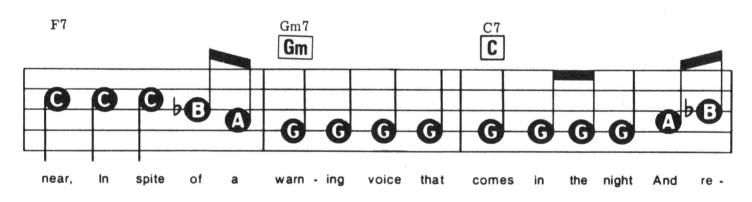

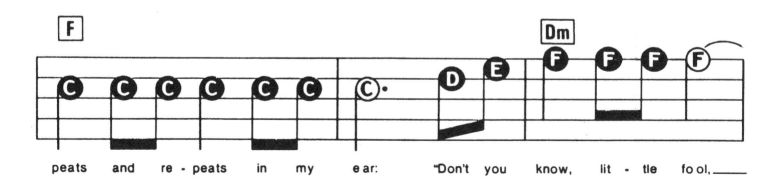

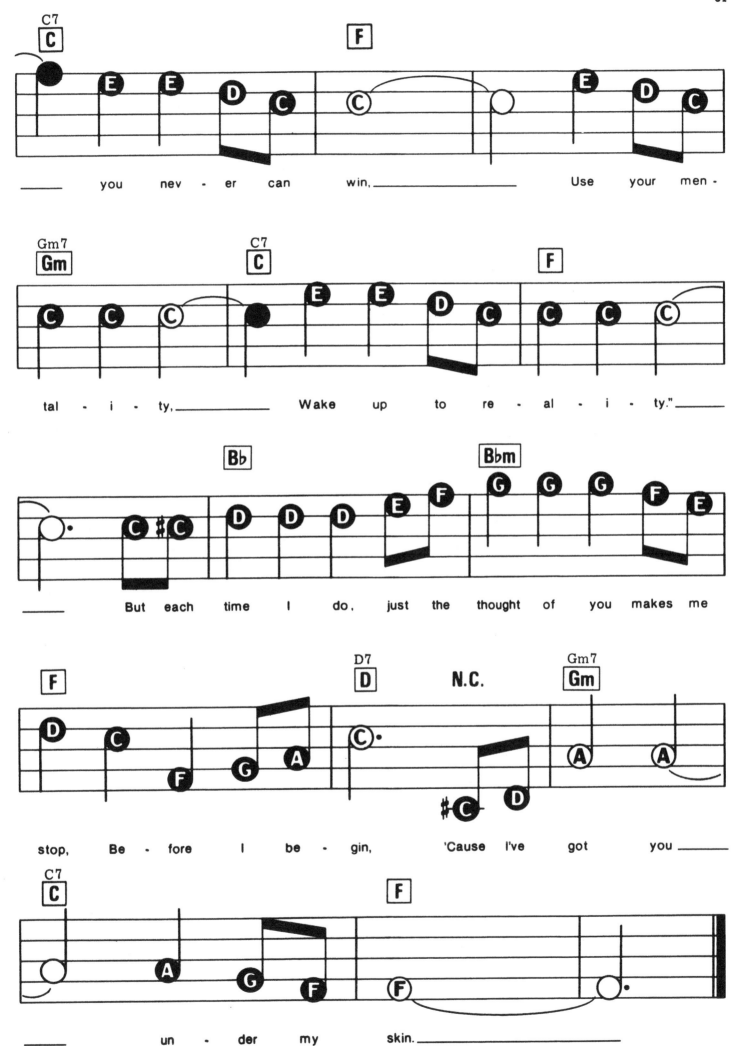

you nev - er can win, _____ Use your men -

tal - i - ty, _____ Wake up to re - al - i - ty." _____

But each time I do, just the thought of you makes me

stop, Be - fore I be - gin, 'Cause I've got you _____

_____ un - der my skin. _____

I Love You
from MEXICAN HAYRIDE

Registration 2
Rhythm: Ballad or Fox Trot

Words and Music by
Cole Porter

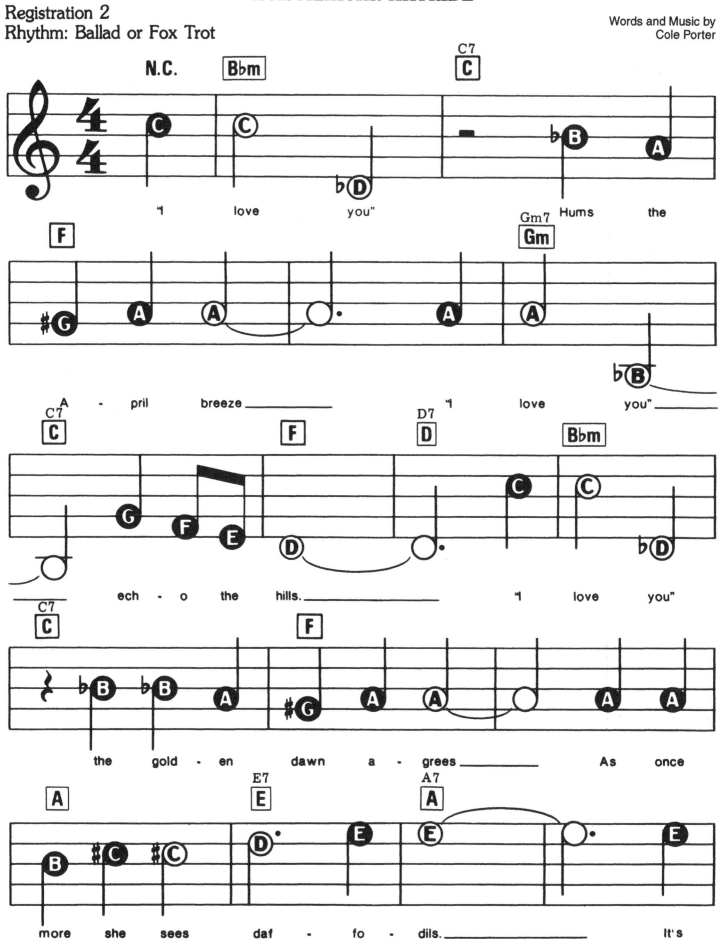

33

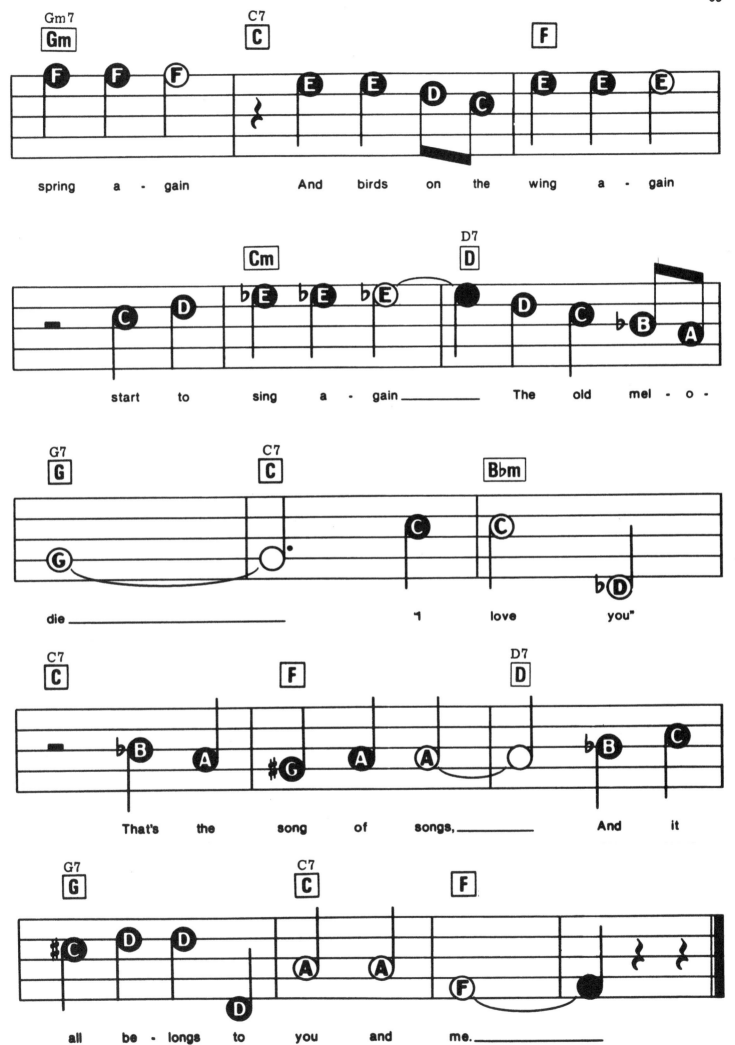

In the Still of the Night
from ROSALIE

Registration 2
Rhythm: Latin

Words and Music by
Cole Porter

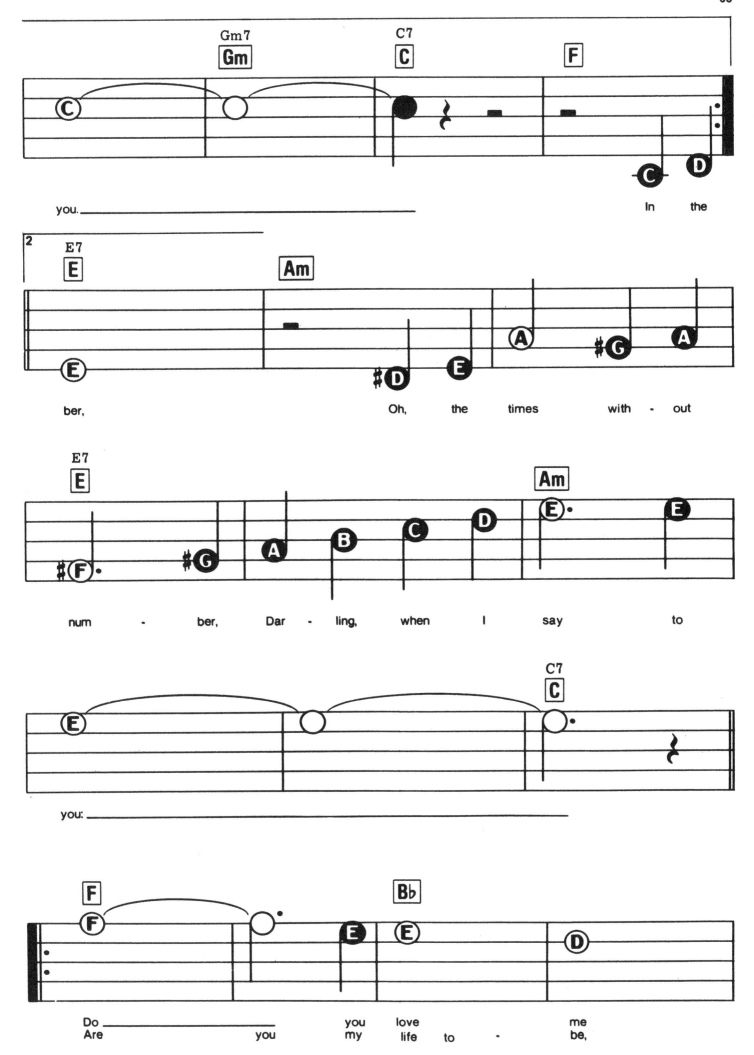

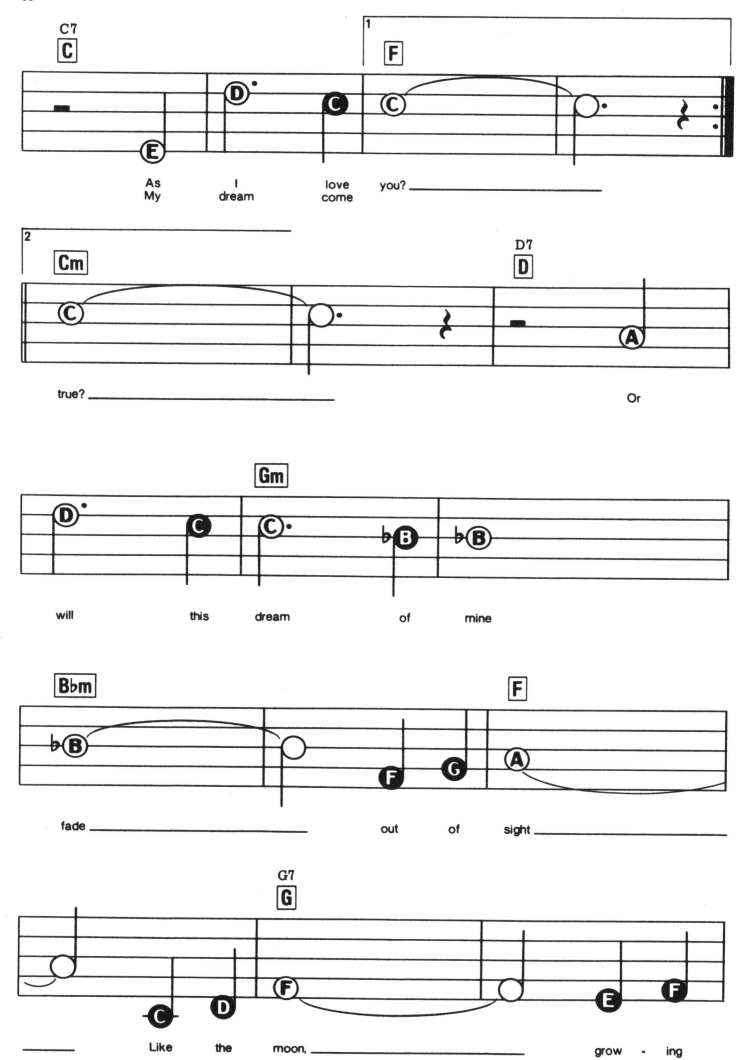

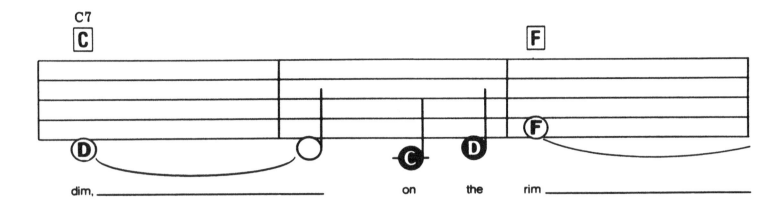

dim, _____ on the rim _____

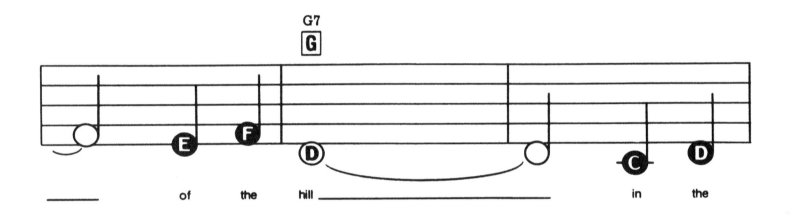

_____ of the hill _____ in the

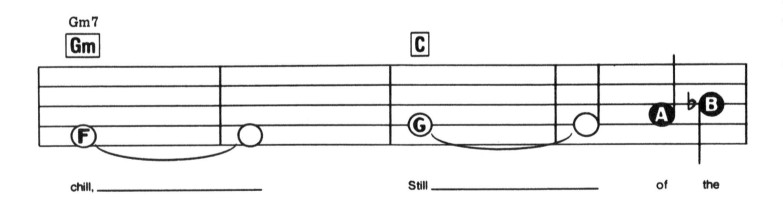

chill, _____ Still _____ of the

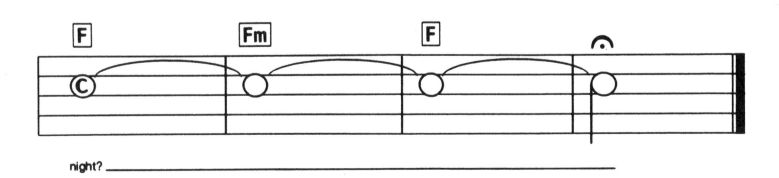

night? _____

It's De-Lovely

from RED, HOT AND BLUE!

Registration 2
Rhythm: Swing

Words and Music by
Cole Porter

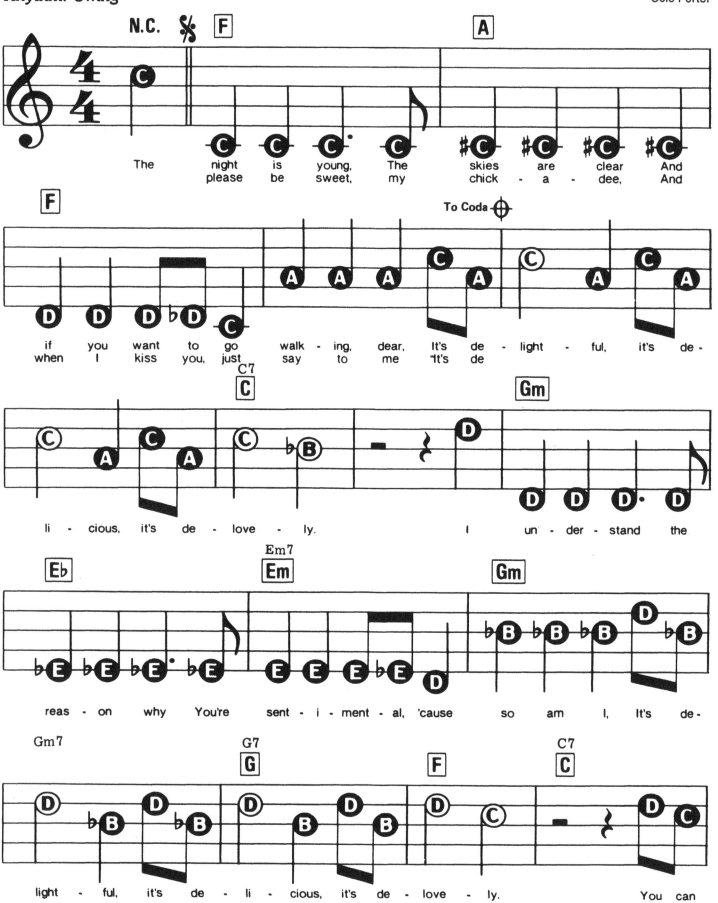

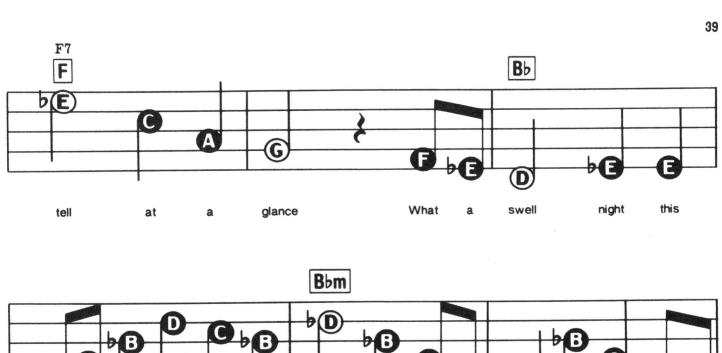

tell   at   a   glance   What   a   swell   night   this

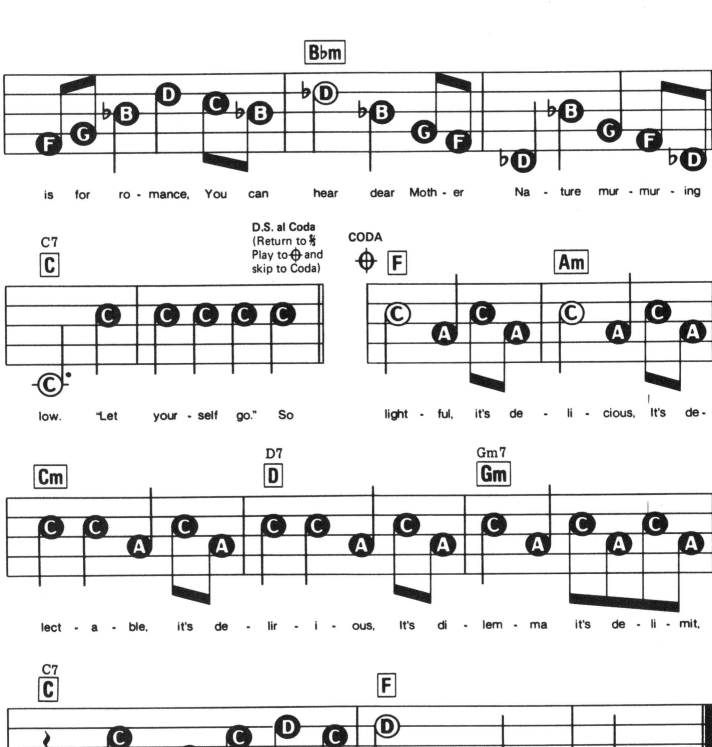

is   for   ro - mance,   You   can   hear   dear   Moth - er   Na - ture   mur - mur - ing

D.S. al Coda
(Return to 𝄋
Play to ⊕ and
skip to Coda)

CODA

low.   "Let   your - self   go."   So   light - ful,   it's   de - li - cious,   It's   de -

lect - a - ble,   it's   de - lir - i - ous,   It's   di - lem - ma   it's   de - li - mit,

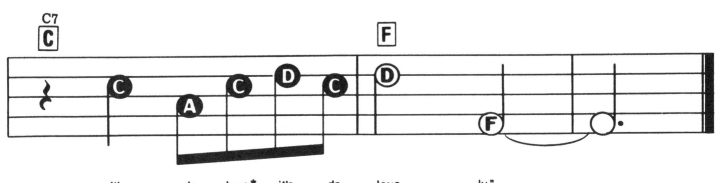

It's   de - luxe,*   it's   de - love - ly." _____

*Pronounced "delukes"

Just One of Those Things

Registration 7
Rhythm: Swing or Jazz

Words and Music by
Cole Porter

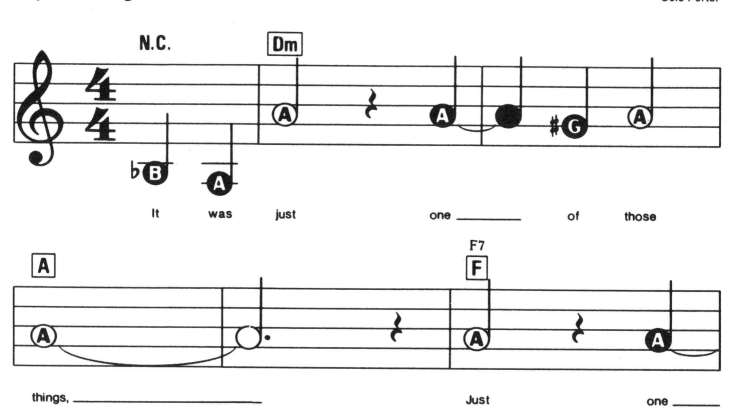

It   was   just   one _____ of   those

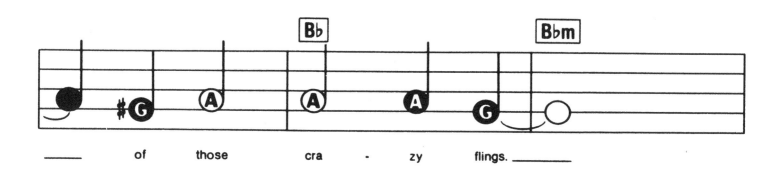

things, _____   Just   one _____

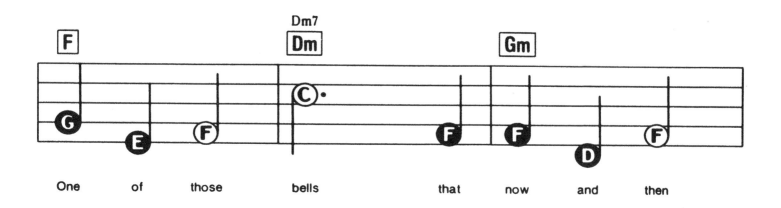

_____   of   those   cra - zy   flings. _____

One   of   those   bells   that   now   and   then

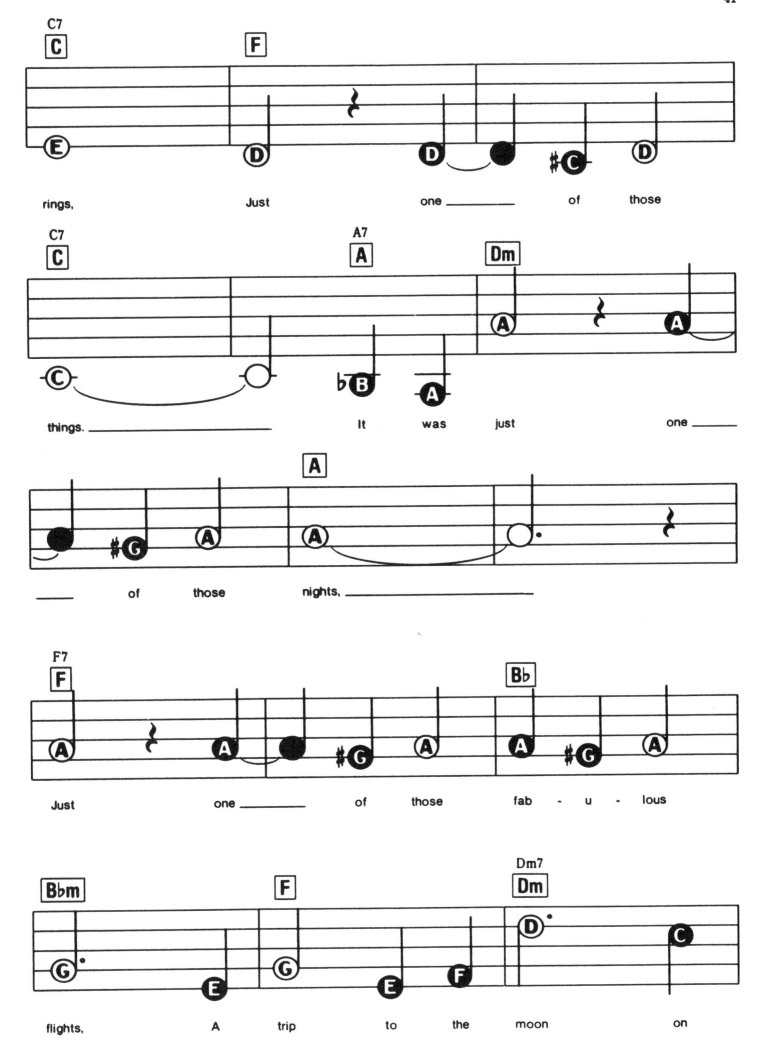

42

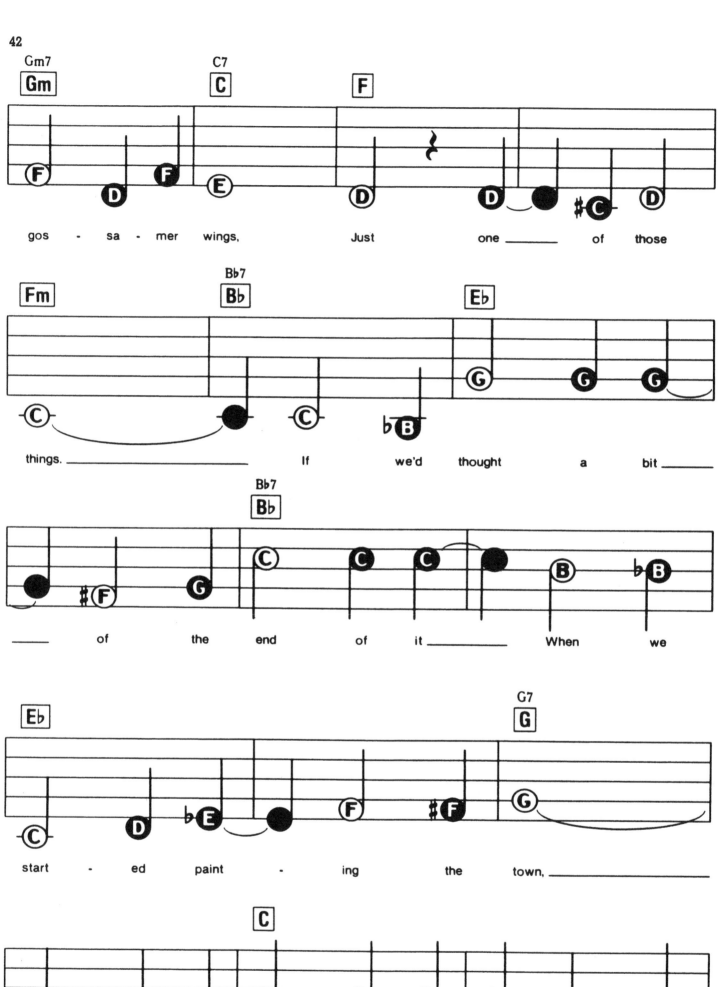

gos - sa - mer wings, Just one _____ of those things. _____ If we'd thought a bit _____ of the end of it _____ When we start - ed paint - ing the town, _____ We'd have been a - ware _____ That our

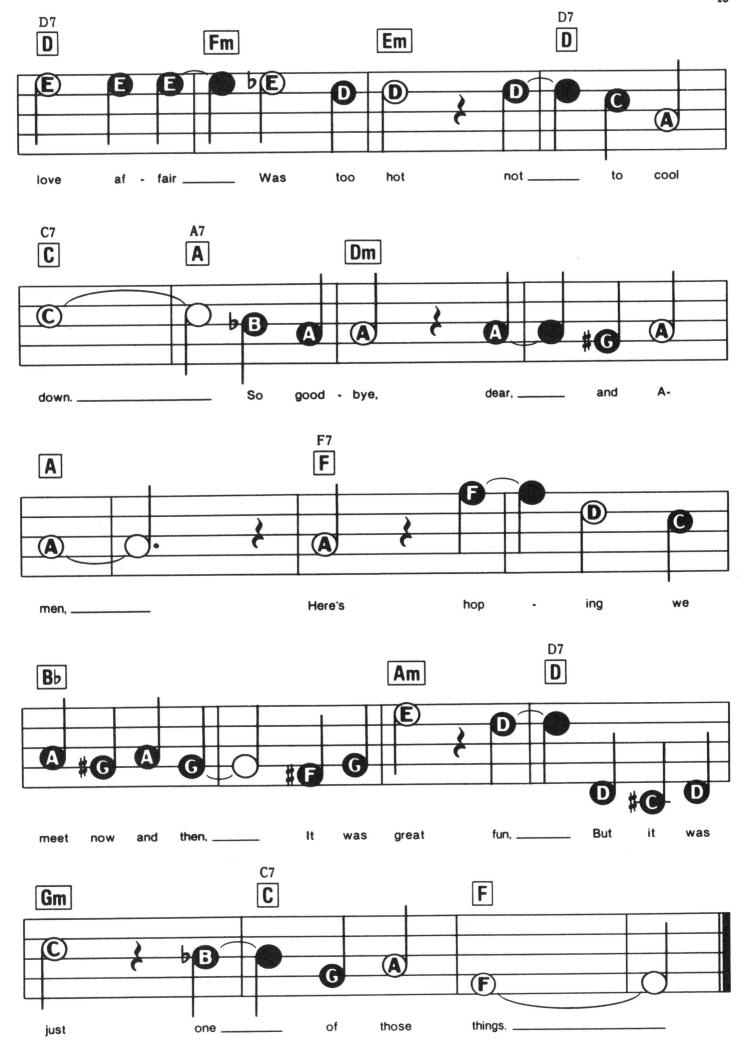

Let's Do It
(Let's Fall in Love)

Registration 4
Rhythm: Fox Trot or Swing

Words and Music by
Cole Porter

Birds do it, Bees do it, E - ven ed - u - cat - ed
spon - ges they say, do it, Oy - sters, down in Oy - ster

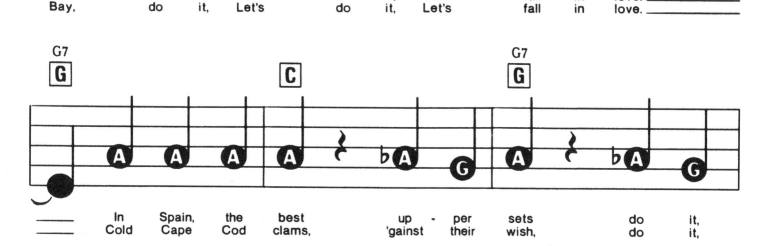

fleas do it, Let's do it, Let's fall in love. _____
Bay, do it, Let's do it, Let's fall in love. _____

_____ In Spain, the best up - per sets do it,
_____ Cold Cape the Cod clams, 'gainst their wish, do it,

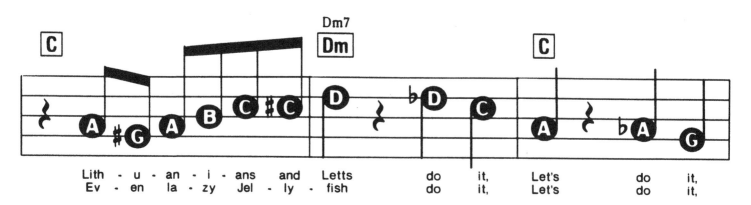

Lith - u - an - i - ans and Letts do it, Let's do it,
Ev - en la - zy Jel - ly - fish do it, Let's do it,

45

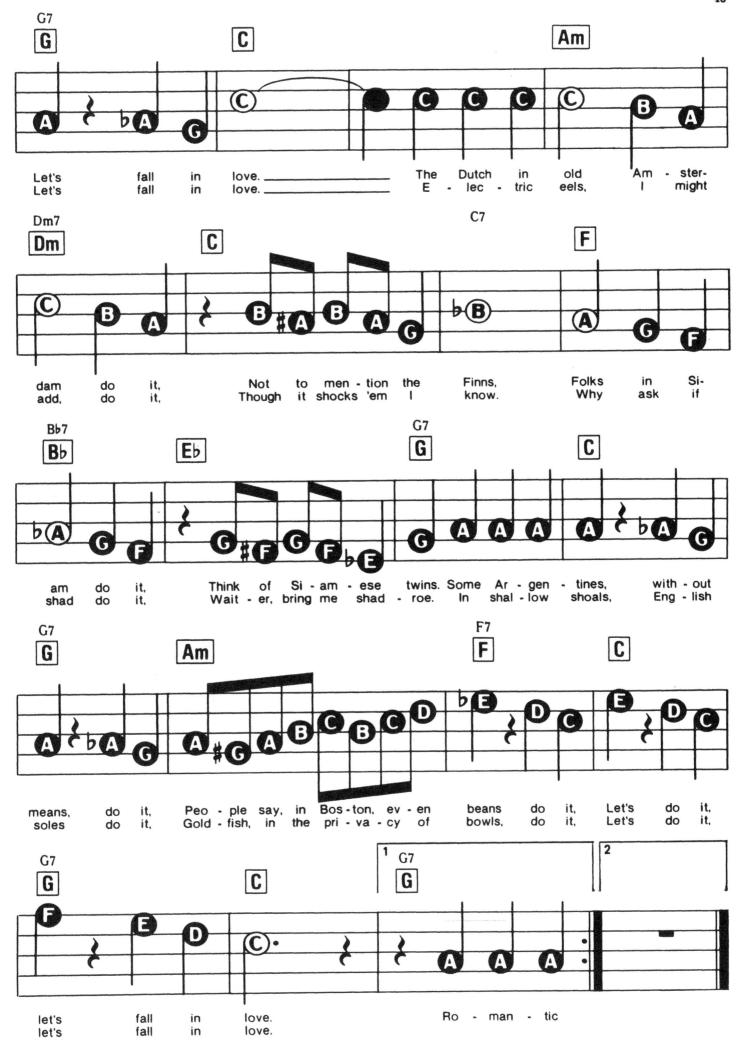

Love for Sale
from THE NEW YORKERS

Registration 9
Rhythm: Swing or Jazz

Words and Music by
Cole Porter

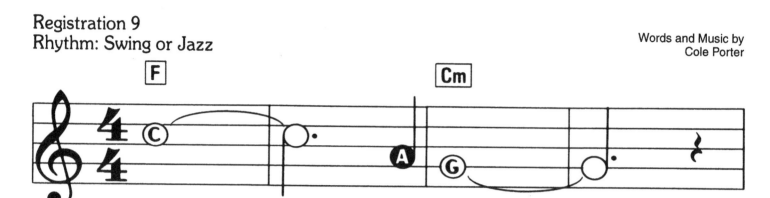

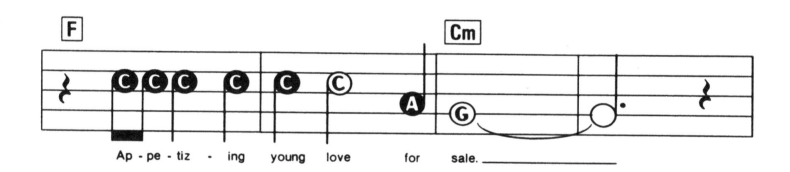

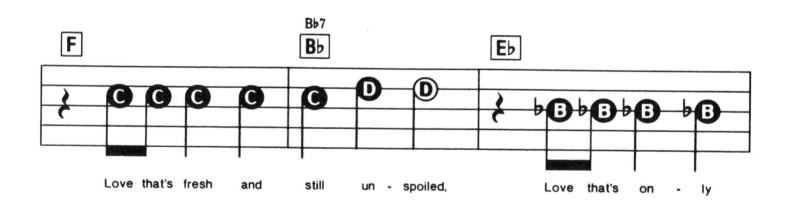

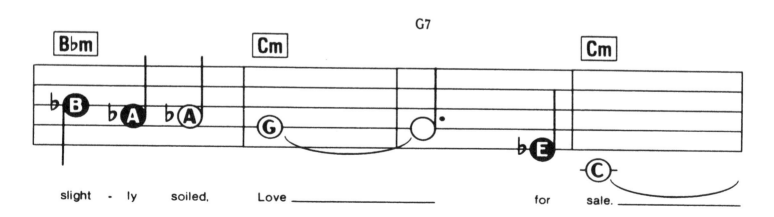

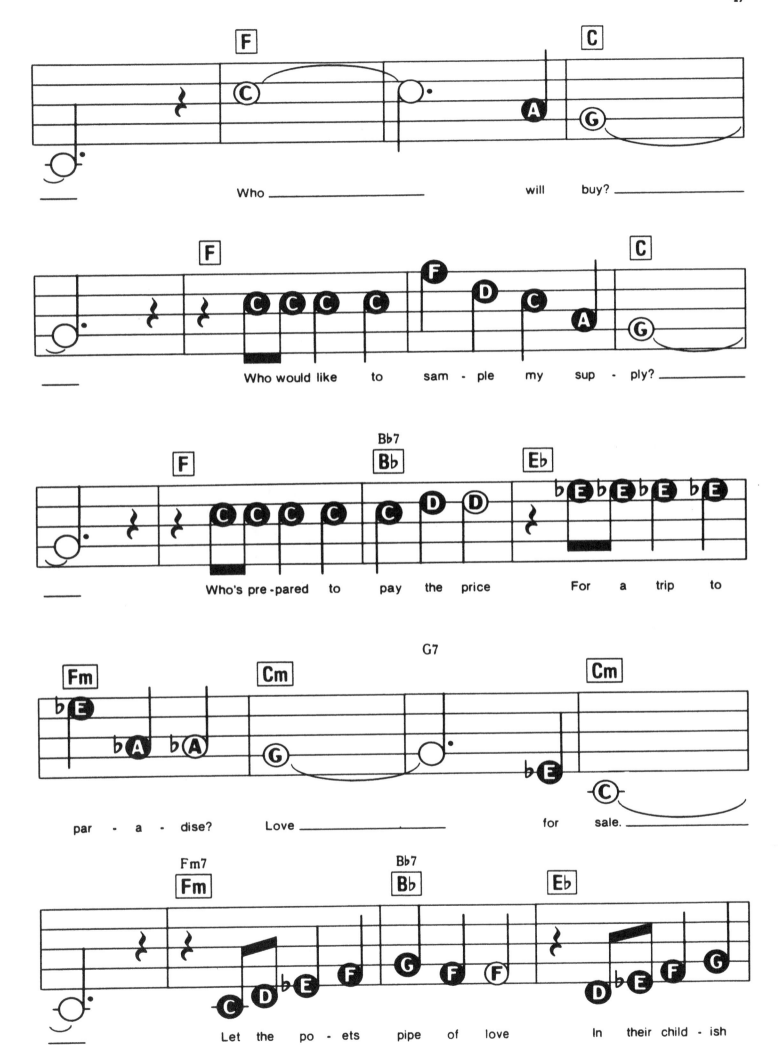

48

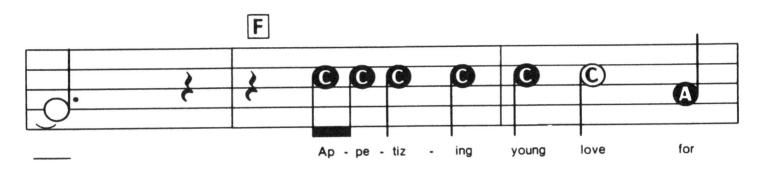

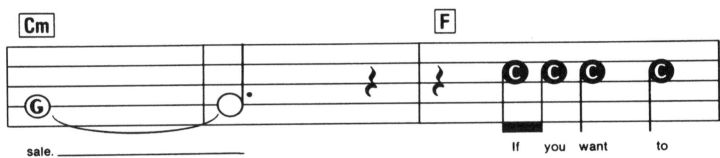

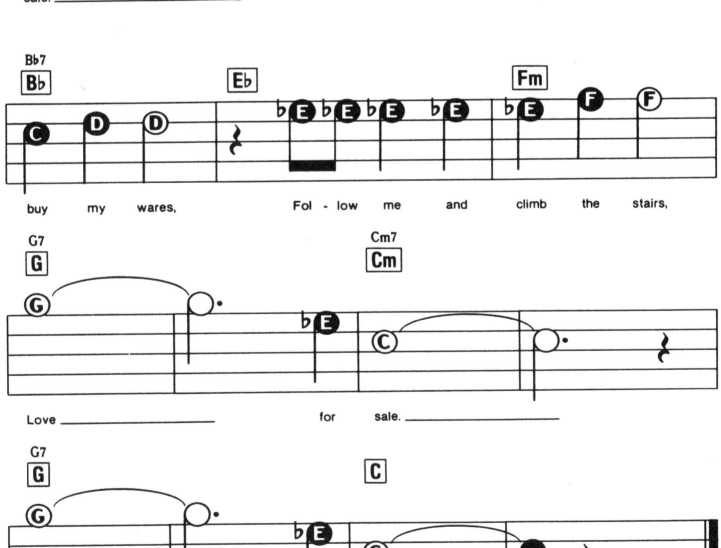

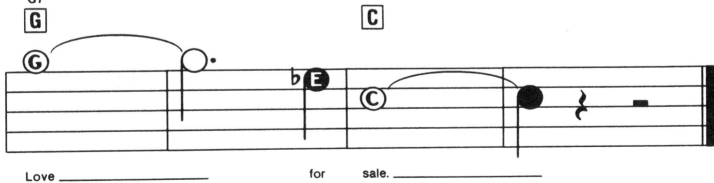

My Heart Belongs to Daddy

from LEAVE IT TO ME

Registration 7
Rhythm: Swing or Jazz

Words and Music by
Cole Porter

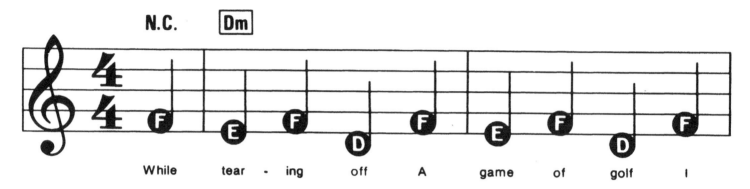

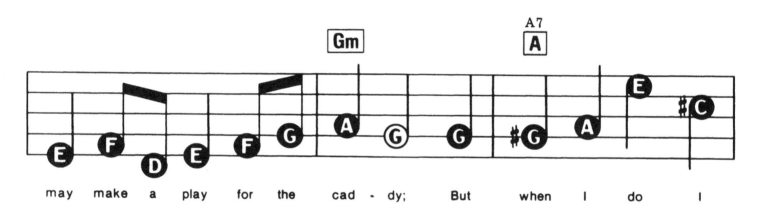

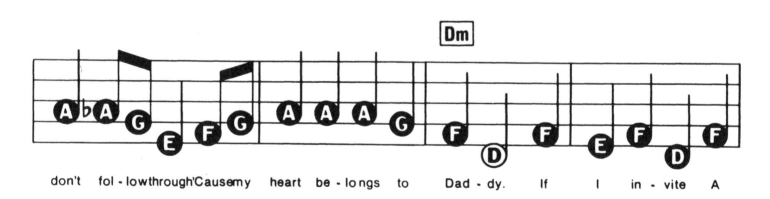

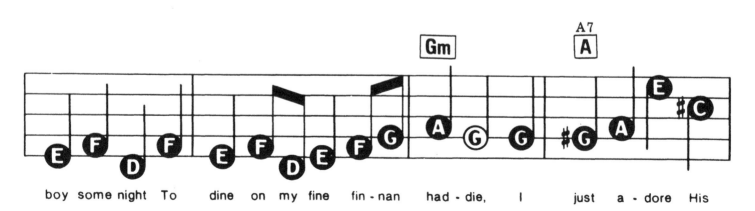

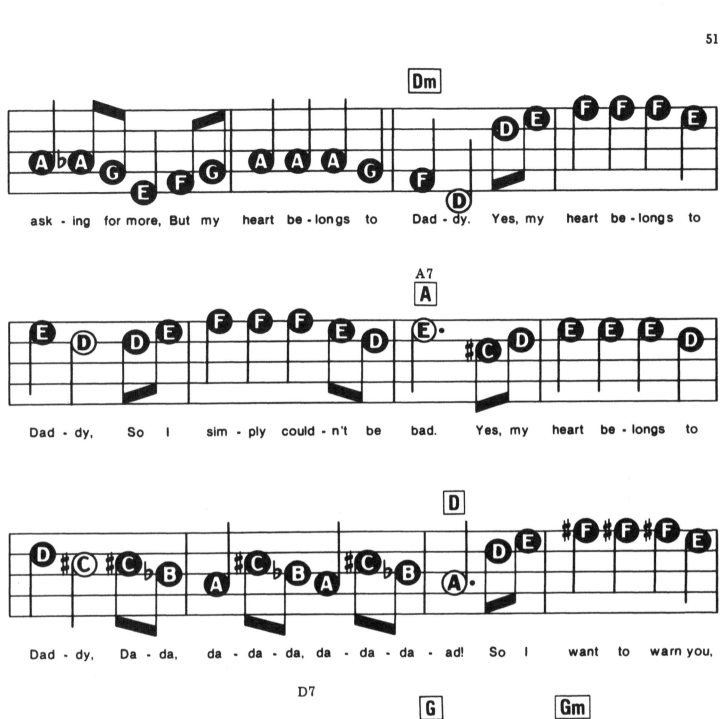

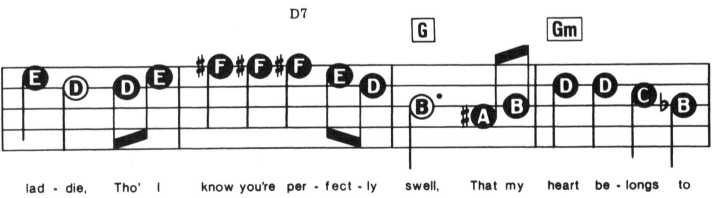

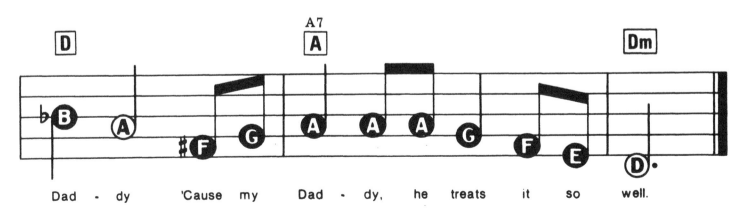

Night and Day

from THE GAY DIVORCE

Registration 7
Rhythm: Fox Trot or Swing

Words and Music by
Cole Porter

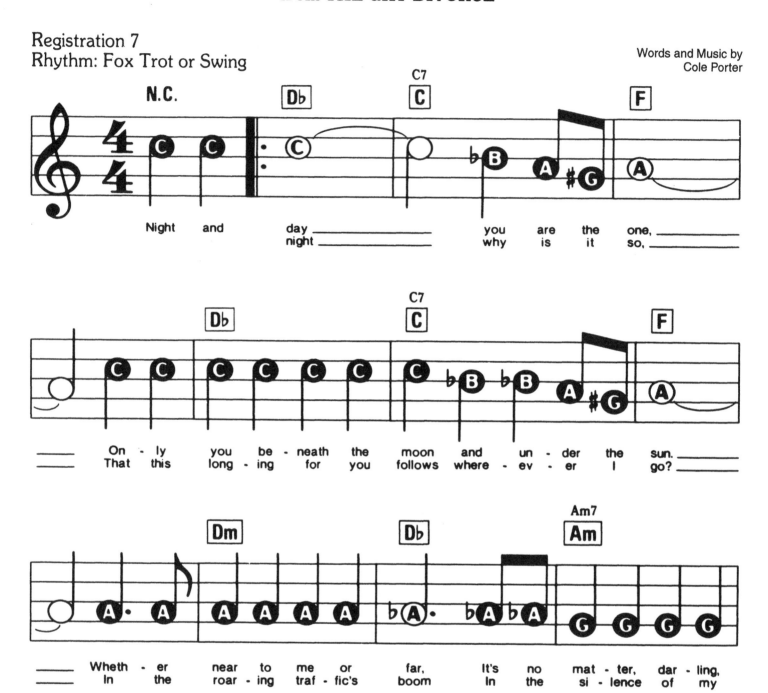

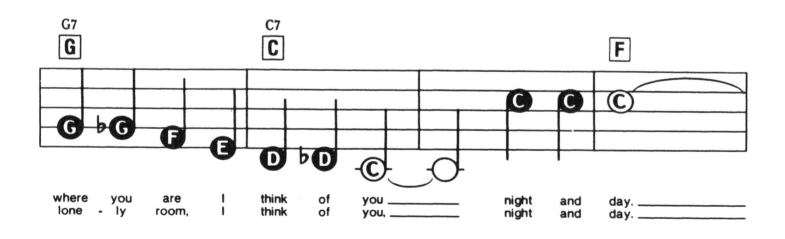

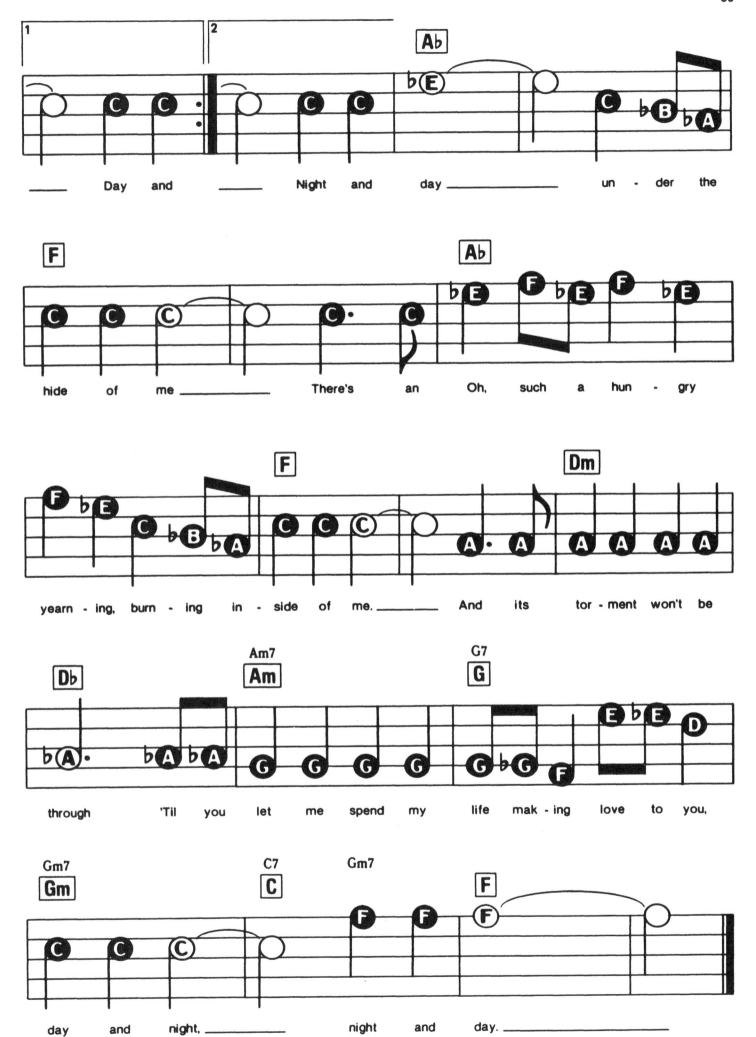

True Love
from HIGH SOCIETY

Registration 4
Rhythm: Waltz

Words and Music by
Cole Porter

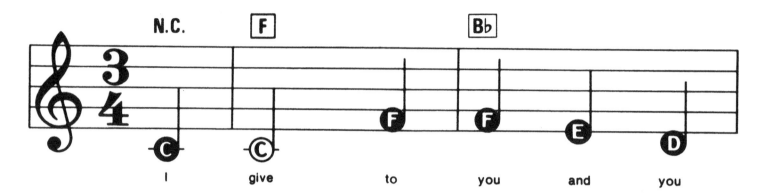

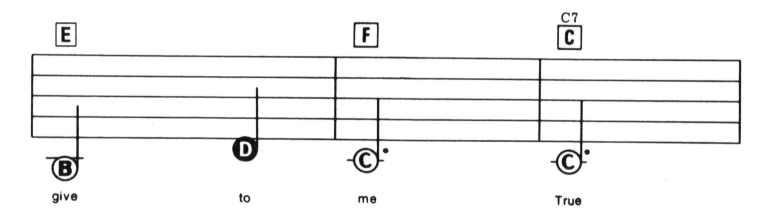

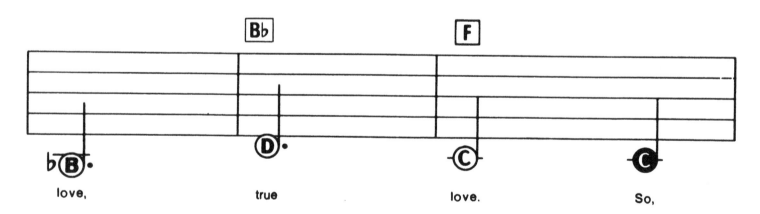

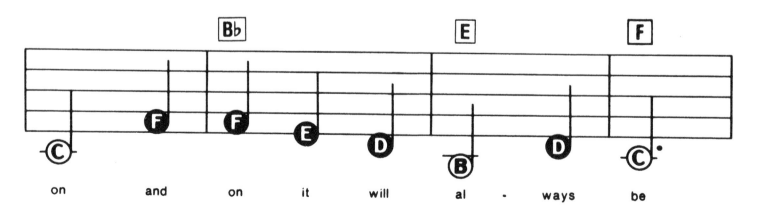

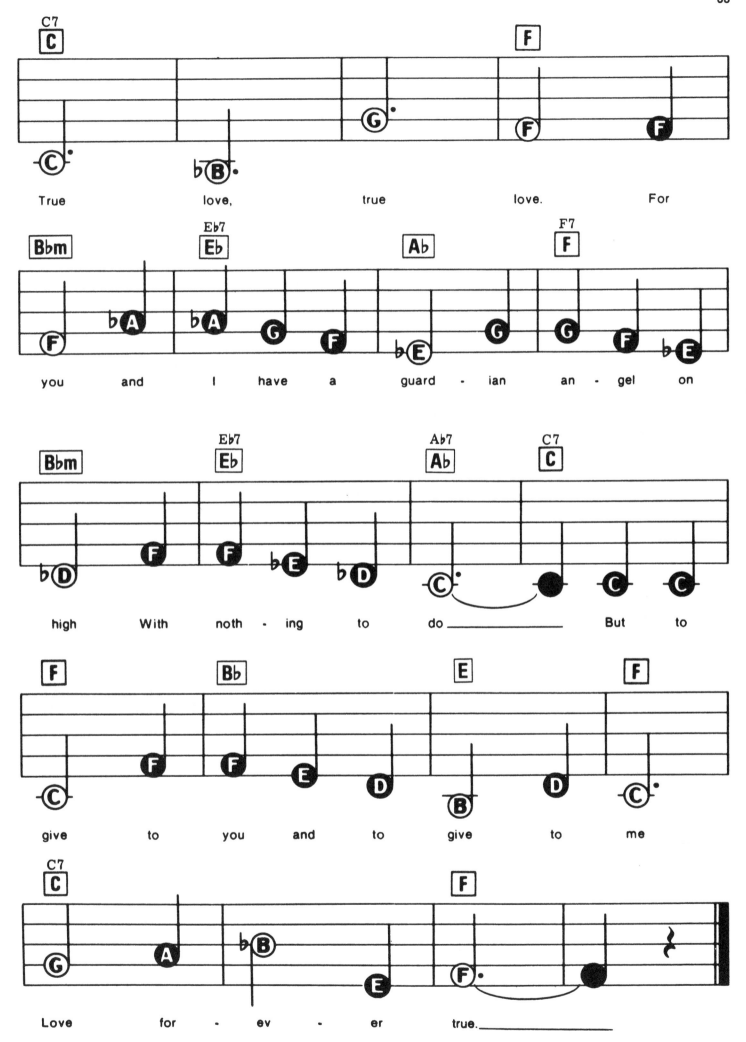

What Is This Thing Called Love?

Registration 7
Rhythm: Fox Trot or Swing

Words and Music by
Cole Porter

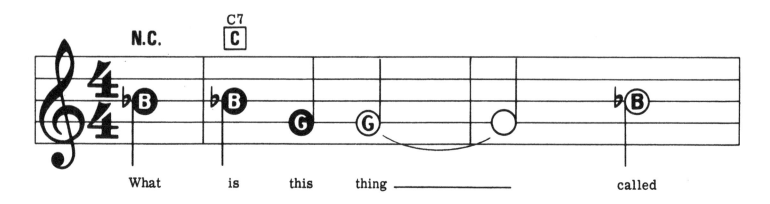

What   is   this   thing _____   called

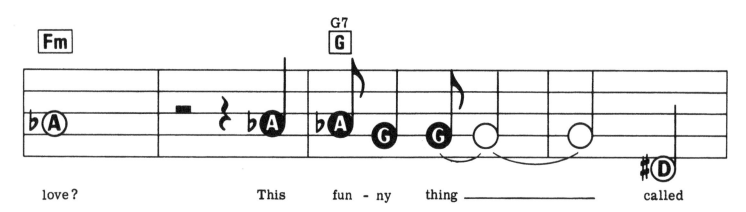

love?   This   fun - ny   thing _____   called

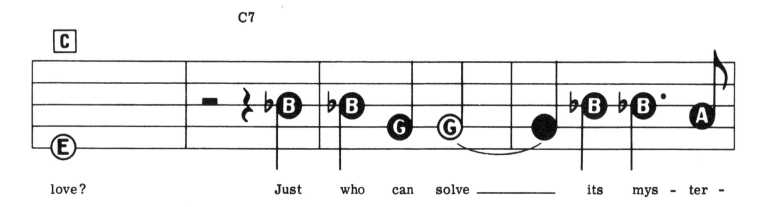

love?   Just   who   can   solve _____   its   mys - ter -

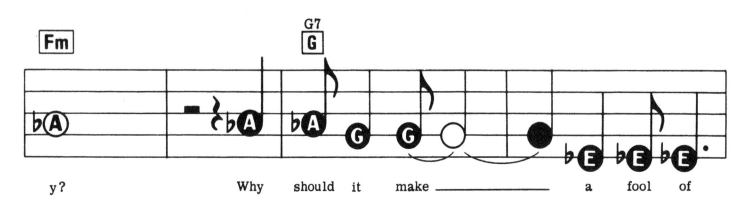

y?   Why   should   it   make _____   a   fool   of

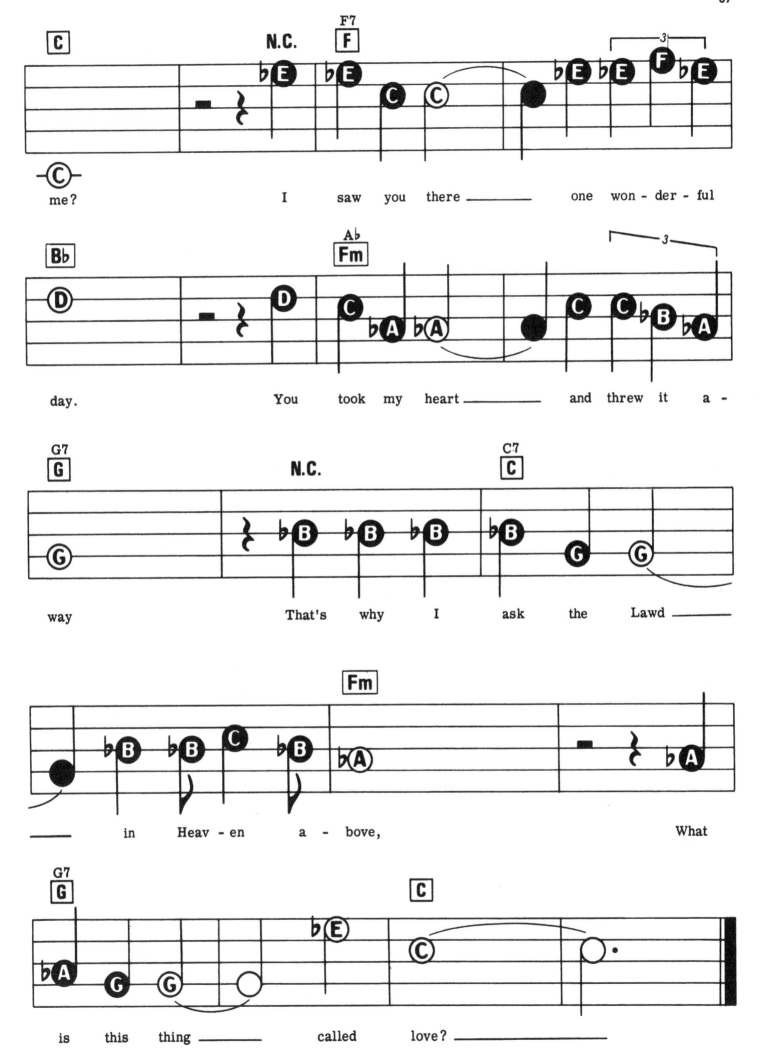

You Do Something to Me
from CAN-CAN

Registration 4
Rhythm: Fox Trot or Swing

Words and Music by
Cole Porter

59

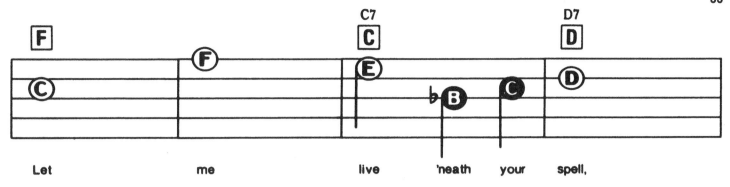

Let me live 'neath your spell,

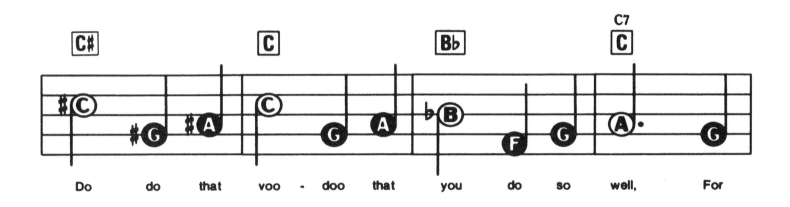

Do do that voo - doo that you do so well, For

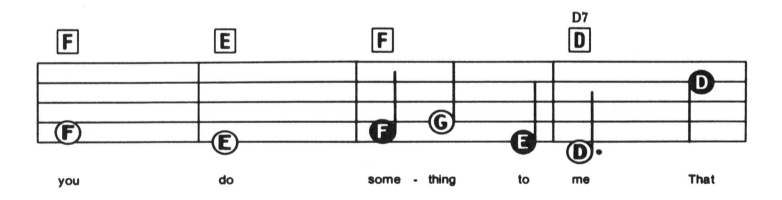

you do some - thing to me That

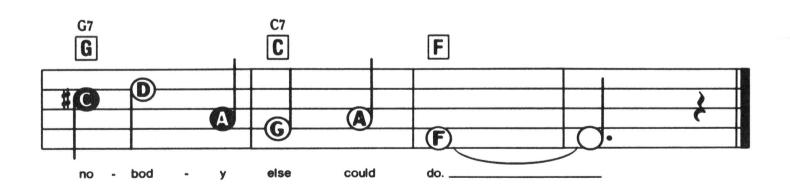

no - bod - y else could do. _____

You'd Be So Nice to Come Home To
from SOMETHING TO SHOUT ABOUT

Registration 9
Rhythm: Swing

Words and Music by
Cole Porter

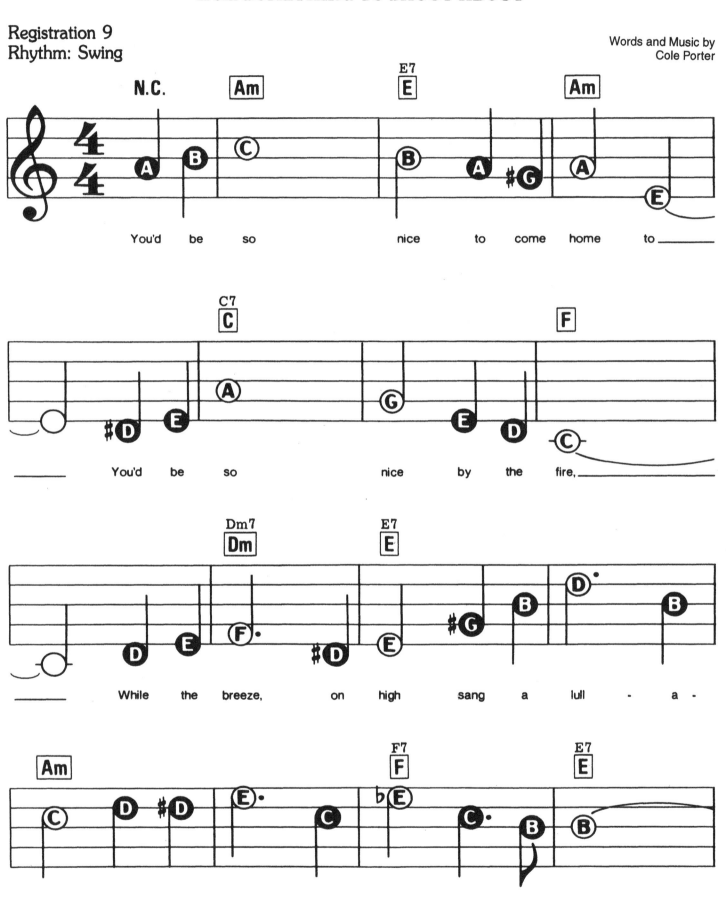

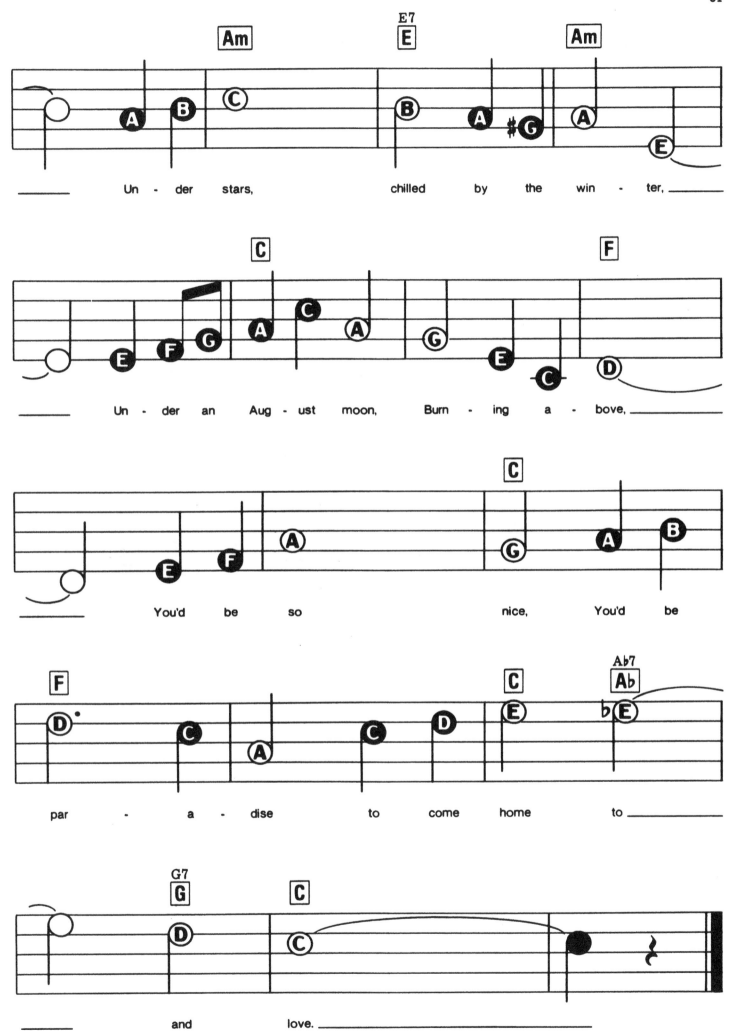

You're the Top
from ANYTHING GOES

Registration 4
Rhythm: Swing or Jazz

Words and Music by
Cole Porter

Registration Guide

- Match the Registration number on the song to the corresponding numbered category below. Select and activate an instrumental sound available on your instrument.
- Choose an automatic rhythm appropriate to the mood and style of the song. (Consult your Owner's Guide for proper operation of automatic rhythm features.)
- Adjust the tempo and volume controls to comfortable settings.

Registration

1	Flute, Pan Flute, Jazz Flute
2	Clarinet, Organ
3	Violin, Strings
4	Brass, Trumpet
5	Synth Ensemble, Accordion, Brass
6	Pipe Organ, Harpsichord
7	Jazz Organ, Vibraphone, Vibes, Electric Piano, Jazz Guitar
8	Piano, Electric Piano
9	Trumpet, Trombone, Clarinet, Saxophone, Oboe
10	Violin, Cello, Strings